MW00533871

LORA O'BRIEN

Irish Witchcraft from an Irish Witch

True to the Heart (Second Edition)

Eel & otter

First published by Eel & Otter Press 2020

Copyright © 2020 by Lora O'Brien

All rights reserved. No part of this publication may be reproduced, stored or transmitted in any form or by any means, electronic, mechanical, photocopying, recording, scanning, or otherwise without written permission from the publisher. It is illegal to copy this book, post it to a website, or distribute it by any other means without permission.

Lora O'Brien asserts the moral right to be identified as the author of this work.

Lora O'Brien has no responsibility for the persistence or accuracy of URLs for external or third-party Internet Websites referred to in this publication and does not guarantee that any content on such Websites is, or will remain, accurate or appropriate.

Eel & Otter Press

Dunmore Road, Waterford,

County Waterford, Republic of Ireland.

www.EelandOtter.net

Second edition

This book was professionally typeset on Reedsy.
Find out more at reedsy.com

To the folk this book originally acknowledged - even though things haven't stayed the same, I wish you well. (And Kane, I'm sorry they spelled your name wrong.)

What has stayed the same, with new branches grown or grafted... is family. My heart, my soul, my life; the strength of the tree.

This one is for Sorrel, Ahlanna, and Conall.

Contents

III   How It Will Be

Foreword

Some Reader Reviews, from the 1st Edition

Ty Bevington - 5 out of 5 stars (2006)

A Wake-up Call!

Lora O'Brien has written a book that is both dead serious in tone and punctuated with her Irish wit. This is not a book for fluffy bunnies, wanna-be's, 'Charmed' fans, et al. This is the experience of a woman who is Irish and a witch, and lives it. She pushes aside layers of blatant and not so blatant misinformation on being Irish and being a witch. While realising we cannot all move to Ireland and pick up the language, we can understand the experience she shares with us on being as authentic as possible.

In a lot of ways, her approach is akin to Ray Buckland in his groundbreaking books, 'The Complete Book of Witchcraft' and 'The Tree'. Buckland had to dispel stereotypes and Rumours of orgies, drug/alcohol consumption, 'black mass', etc. As that has largely been cleared away thru the pagan/witch community, the new stereotypes-instant gratification, fancy, meaningless titles, spinning 'burning times' icons, and using magick indiscriminately have to be dispelled to see the real soul of the Witch-not the trappings of 'Pentacles, Inc.'

O'Brien covers sabbats, stages of the Witch's life, persecution, sacred sites, and deities. This book is a serious look at herself, her tradition and her future. It's also worth a look as your future, too.

I cannot recommend this book enough. If you are a serious witch, you'll see some of yourself here and find new doors in your soul to explore. If you are looking to become a serious witch, and are ready to drop the party games, this book will help you map your escape route. I read a lot of books. I attend lectures, teach, and just chat with others about our faith and craft. This book is destined to become a modern classic. You may not agree with everything, but you've got a real friend in this opus.

J. Healis - 5 out of 5 stars (2015)

Certainly not 'Wicca with Shamrocks'

This is such a refreshing and inspirational take on understanding what it is to be a witch. O'Brien gets to the point and lets readers know that this is not the fluffy path of new agers, and that being a witch takes work and dedication to understanding the world around you. She lets people know that you can just pick and choose what you like and don't like until you understand the significance of all aspects of witchcraft. New Age Wiccans are apt to call themselves 'eclectic' when, it seems, they just don't want to make the effort to know why some things work for them, and some don't.

O'Brien makes things simple for the reader: know the history, know the things from which you draw power, understand why we celebrate certain times and not others, and make this a part of your everyday life.

Reading this book has focused my path and given me better understanding of what I need to learn, and what I didn't know. For me, in this book, O'Brien was like the teacher who said, 'forget all those books; go out and learn what it's really about'. If I ever get the chance to thank her in person, I will happily buy the pints.

Irish-American Witchcraft: Top 5 favourite Witchcraft Authors

[Patheos Pagan Article] by Morgan Daimler (2019)

I read O'Brien's 'Irish Witchcraft from an Irish Witch' in the mid-00's when it came out, and that as well as the later book 'A Practical Guide to Irish Spirituality', and found both to be essential in shaping my personal practice.

It's no secret that I started in neopagan witchcraft in the early 90's, segued into Celtic Reconstructionism with an Irish focus in the later 90's, and by the later 2000's had moved into a witchcraft that incorporated aspects of Reconstructionism with the fairy faith.

But prior to reading *Irish Witchcraft From An Irish Witch* I had always kept my CR and my witchcraft compartmentalised, something that caused me a lot of unhappiness if I'm being honest; it was this book and its follow up that began opening my eyes to the idea that it was possible to find a respectful way to blend all of the aspects of my spirituality into a cohesive whole.

Preface

Oh this book.

It's the end of 2018 as I write this preface, and I've had the publishing rights back from the original publisher for quite a while. To be honest, I've been dragging my heels on getting it in print again, despite it being one of the most frequent requests I get.

Don't get me wrong, I don't hate it or anything. It's just, I was so VERY young when I wrote it. 26 years old when it was first published, and in such a different place in my life. Of course I've grown and changed since then. Of course my personal practice has changed significantly... it would be really weird and kinda sad if it hadn't, right?

Going deeper into the original lore of Ireland gave me a connection I didn't have then, even after growing up here and wading through the magic of Ireland my whole life. Digging through digital manuscripts and academic papers and books that weighed more than my kids did, all gave me an insight that shifted my personal practice into a thing that is almost a part of the land itself. And then I spent a good number of years working professionally as a Guardian (manager, they called it, but whatever) at Cruachán - Rathcroghan - and that changed me even more.

So yeah. I'm in a different place right now.

For a long time it made me ashamed of this work. Like I'd done something wrong, or at least - not good enough - in writing it. I mean, that probably says as much about my mental state and issues back then as it did about anything else, but there you go.

I began to travel to teach, and people would rave at me about how this book changed their perspective, their practice, their life. And I'd be mortified, because I thought I should have written it so much better, helped them so much more.

Until one of those conversations that stops you in your tracks, or maybe derails you a little. But in a good way, because the tracks were laid all wrong. I met a woman called Victoria at PantheaCon in California, my first year out there, and after a long day of feeling that embarrassment as folks talked about this book, I confessed to her that I didn't like it. That I should have done better. That I'd like to take it back and re-write it completely.

An' you know what she said to me?

'You were where you were, back then. And there's plenty of people who need that book as it is, because they are still there right now'.

Now, I'm paraphrasing there. But that was the gist of it. And it floored me. Because that's exactly why I wrote this book in the first place.

I didn't want to be an author. I didn't want to be well known, or in any way... responsible for people. *shudders*

But I wrote the book I had needed, ten years before; when I was 15, and seeking, and desperate for something that felt right and REAL to me as an Irish person, and all I could find were foreign voices, foreign spiritual systems, foreign magic, to try to express or explain the things I had felt and experienced and known - deep down - all of my life.

So I'm putting this book back together, with an updated resource section, a few corrections to the text, some small additions or notes for clarification, but essentially - it's the same book. I'll get a fresh round of folk complaining in the reviews that I'm too grumpy or snarky, that I'm expecting too much by saying they should *GASP* make a Godsdamn effort to learn the language of the culture they are gaining from, and that the book doesn't suit them for various reasons of their own devising. Fuck it, and fuck them.

This one is for you folks who are still coming ashore from almost drowning in a sea of 'Celtic' NeoPagan shite. There's a lot more work you can do, if this suits you, and you develop a *grá* for Ireland. Consider this… a bridge; between that, and authentic Irish Paganism.

Check those resources (there's so much more available now, it's a pleasure to recommend them!), visit my own website LoraOBrien.ie for the blog, the other books I've written. Go and find the classes I teach at the IrishPaganSchool.com. There are Guided Journeys at the School too, a whole unique native Journeying system in fact, there's a Guided Meditation Membership for a regular download of Journeying resources.

You have options now that we didn't have when this book first came out, and that I certainly didn't have back in the 90s in Ireland when I was starting out. Make good use of them! Enjoy them!

I'm not embarrassed anymore, to include this book among them.

It's good enough.

Acknowledgement

For Victoria (and Ray!) Danger.

Thanks for helping me get my initial shit together enough to begin work on the 2nd edition of this book.

Dainséar Abú!

ALL THAT WE MUST LEAVE BEHIND

She Stands
   Silent, hooded, darkened countenance
   shifting, muted, inescapably There.
   Her Face
   Unknowable, terrible, hidden
   She is Everything and Nothing.
   Two Spears
   Weapons of truth, Imperative
   Thrusting knowledge and awareness
   Slaying
   All that we must leave behind
   Forcing
   All that we must discover
   Darkness and Strength
   Power and Insight
   Fear and Finding
   She Stands
   Connected, terrified, thrilled
   Facing the Great Queen
   Back into her own,
   coming home.

Lora O'Brien, *Bealtaine* 2004.

To Begin

Lora O'Brien, Irish Priest and Witch. That's the title I choose when I have to describe what I am or what I do; not Wiccan, not Alexandrian, not Thelemite, not High Priestess of Crow Coven. Irish, Priest (or Priestess), Witch. Each word means something to me. They are the only words that matter to me when describing what I am, in a magical sense.

Mother, partner, body-piercer, entrepreneur, writer, daughter, sister – they all have their place in my life. But magically speaking, for me, it's about being Irish, and exploring that connection. Connecting with my ancestors, my land, my heritage. It's about being a Priest, carrying the old ways forward and working within those traditions. Being a voice and a point of contact within the community for those who are seeking, while I continue to seek myself. And being a Witch, *Bean Draoí* (pron. Ban-Dree) or *Draoí* as I call it now, in more gender fluid terms… a practitioner and user of the magic that surrounds (and is part of) us all, a walker between the worlds.

Aleister Crowley said that magic is the "science and art of causing change to occur in conformity with Will". This sounds about right to me, taking into account that we can manipulate the natural energies that permeate the Universe.

These three things are important to me – connecting, helping and utilising the magic – Irish, Priest, and Witch. None of them were conferred upon or presented to me by anybody else; they each hold self-discovered relevance for me while I walk this path. Each is linked intrinsically to the core of who and what I am, and what I aspire to be. And I do continue to learn and grow into each of these things, because you are never finished: the day you feel you know enough is the day to give it all up.

But this book is not about me. All I can do is share one person's experiences on their own path, not tell you how to walk yours. If a guru is what you are looking for, find another book! If I am a teacher, it is because I am already walking the path that you, Dear Reader, may wish to be on. Although each of us must make our own way, I can put up signposts at least, and make the way slightly less hazardous for those who wish to walk a similar path.

This is Not Wicca?

One thing I was determined not to give you here is the sort of 'Wicca with Shamrocks', as a dear friend of mine put it (in her usual succinct way), that is often seen in the New Age scene. Throwing the names Lugh and Brighid into the mix – instead of the more usual Cernunnos and Aradia – in an otherwise Wiccan circle, does not an Irish Witch nor Irish Witchcraft make. I have defined a Witch as a user of the magic that surrounds and is part of us all, and that's relevant for anyone who chooses to use the term. I feel strongly that Witchcraft and Wicca are different things. What then does a Wiccan do that is different?

In my dealings with newcomers to the Craft, the difference between Witchcraft and Wicca has been one of the most often asked questions, so, although it's not strictly concerned with my Irish heritage and learning, I do feel it needs to be addressed in this book - as we will fall into the 'New Age' category. A lot of books use the terms interchangeably - all Witches are Wiccan and vice versa - but this immediately cuts off so many who are Witches, yet are not religious (or don't identify as Pagan, at least). It also presumes all Wiccans use magic and spells. Not true. Although there is crossover in a lot of cases, and blending of the two paths, they are in many other cases two very different things.

It has been said by many of the Craft's older generation that we now have a spoiled generation of Witches; in their day, there was no Internet, very few books available, and very little source material of any description for newcomers to Craft. We certainly are spoiled for choice. A plethora of books, websites, TV shows – varying in standard from the profound to the ludicrous – are currently available to anybody who wants to 'be a Witch'.

We might indeed have many spoiled Witches running around, but we also have some rather confused ones. The Craft has become so diverse, so broken down by all the garbage that has been marketed as fact, that not even the loose standards or norms that the original Wiccan path finders took as their rights hold true for a lot of modern seekers: including, for example, the original usage and meanings of the words (Wiccan and Wicca only grew popular in the 1970s).

Gardner himself only used the word Wicca rarely, and preferred to call himself Witch, whereas in today's world of such diverse practices, the need is being keenly felt for a modern definition of the terms as they are being used today. Serious seekers are floundering in a sea of raving authors and misconception-made-truth. Wicca is being diluted beyond all recognition by eclectic fluffies who do have the dreaded pick and mix attitude to religion. This seems especially true in the United States, where serious and practical Wiccans often find themselves lumped in with the not so serious; ridiculed, and reviled, often through sheer ignorance that Wicca can be anything more than what the teenage queens and fairy-focused airheads deem it to be.

Among the Craft folk themselves, there are also major problems. For too long there was a tendency amongst some circles to look down upon others as not 'properly' initiated, lacking in lineage, or adherents of an inferior tradition. I abhor any "you're not properly initiated, my coven is better than your coven" type arguments, but I do feel it is important to acknowledge that some follow an initiatory tradition, and some don't.

It does not make one better than the other: they are simply different – with different aims, different goals, and different practitioners. I have often found that it is those who don't follow an initiatory tradition (such as traditional Wicca) who bang on about supposed patronising attitudes or looking down your nose at us non-initiates the loudest, when it's not, in fact, coming from folks within those initiatory traditions at all. Most folks who have been initiated rarely speak of it, and even more rarely make reference to their rank within a tradition.

I make a serious attempt to define the different labels, titles, and options available to newcomers today in the context of modern Craft. Not to be divisive, but to define as clearly as possible how this day's Witches and Wiccans are actually using the terms and titles. Witchcraft is changing; the up and coming generation has changed it beyond belief, even to somebody who was trained as relatively freshly as I, when I first wrote this book. People are going to pick and choose what they call themselves, as it is human nature to define and relate – I am simply trying to give an updated version of definitions as I have encountered them. And this means that not all Witches are Wiccan Witches, and not all who claim themselves Wiccans are actually following a Wiccan way, in the truest sense. This is why I am attempting to re-format and state clearly what it actually takes to be a Wiccan, while not falling into the trap of fundamentalism or one-upmanship.

I will reiterate, just to make this crystal clear: no group, individual, tradition, or way of walking this path is better or more valid than any other. They are just different. Most newcomers are very far from ever working in groups - training groups, that is, as I had the good fortune to find when I did. The traditional Wiccan coven is becoming a rare breed indeed, in Ireland at least. With nobody to talk to about these differences, and only outdated books to refer to, newcomers are finding things very confusing and even off-putting from the start. I hope this helps.

This is Wicca

Wicca is a religion, either invented, reconstructed, or published to the world (depending on your point of view) by a man called Gerald Brousseau Gardner (GBG). Although there are elements of ancient heritage contained in Wicca, they are interspersed with the writings and practices of others such as Aleister Crowley and Madame Blavatsky, as well as with ritual magic traditions of Masonic and other orders, and even with the works and ideas of Romantic poets and writers of the 19th century. I highly recommend the work of Philip Heselton for the full historical insight.

Gardner was an initiated member of the O.T.O. (Ordo Templi Orientis, or Order of the Temple of the East) and much of the Wiccan ritual, especially that of the third degree and 'Great Rite' itself, is heavily influenced by the

Gnostic Mass, a primary ritual of the O.T.O.

Gardner – with the help of his priestess, Doreen Valiente, and many other members and friends – wove what is still a very workable system from the bits of magical and cultural traditions that he perceived at the time to be relevant. He formed his own coven in 1951, when the law against Witchcraft was repealed in England. They created what is now known as the Gardnerian Book of Shadows, which a lot of Wiccans still base their practices on.

For modern Wiccans, it can be quite tough to define their practices. Wicca has become a bit of a melting pot for anybody who wants to take a pinch of this and a bit of that, throw it all together with some Egyptian sounding names, and voilá: you are an 'eclectic Wiccan'. The term eclectic has become a refuge for the type of person who takes what they want, when they want (we now call this cultural appropriation), and heaven forbid they have to do any real work - let's all prance about and talk to fairies while waving smudge sticks at each other. I am sure we all know the sort I mean, having perhaps tripped over them sprawled out under the sky while we were on our own merry way to doing some actual Craft work.

I am just about to make myself vastly unpopular by stating that these eclectic mixes do not make you Wiccan. Wicca is a fairly specific belief system with certain criteria that should be mostly met before you could, in good faith and honesty, use the label Wiccan. The criteria are as follows.

Belief in the Duality of Deity (Gods)

More simply, this is a belief in a Goddess and a God, or at least a roughly male and female Force, as a matched pair - duotheism. Polarity is important in Wicca: light and dark, night and day, creation and destruction, male and female. Most Wiccans strive for balance in all things. A lot of Wiccans, and indeed Witches, believe that the Universe is formed from, and every living thing contains, Energy. Although each deity is a distinct and autonomous Being... at the most basic level, all Gods are one God, as they (and we) all return eventually to this Energy.

Belief in Duality of Deity doesn't have to mean specifically worshipping

Lugh and Brighid, or Isis and Osiris, or Zeus and Hera. It doesn't have to mean worshipping anything. I take it to mean believing in (recognising they are there and workable), and having a relationship with, opposing but balancing Energies which are formed from the stuff of the Universe, the same stuff that we are formed from. Some Wiccans do indeed shape, and worship their Gods and Goddesses, according to what pantheon (set of deities from a particular culture) they feel most attuned to.

Although duotheism is the most popular for Wicca, especially when you are starting out, polytheism (belief in multiple deities) or pantheism (belief that the divine is present in everything) are what many grow into. Faith in deity is a very personal thing, and really tough to generalise about! To some people the Gods have distinct personalities and are useful to get in touch with for certain things; for example, if you want to appeal to the Goddess of poetry, the eternal muse, you could address Brighid from the Irish pantheon, or if you needed some help with love you could appeal to Aphrodite of the Greeks.

This suits most Wiccans in the use of ritual, as they can design their workings to fit with particular deity; others keep things more generic and non-specific (for example, Great Earth Goddess, Mother of all things). The single defining factor in this myriad practice is the belief in essentially two balancing energies, possibly descending from one ultimate Source, who/that exist on a different level to that which we mere mortals normally inhabit, who/that are viewed as masculine and feminine – though this does not mean strictly man and woman, it can be taken as cultural norms or traditions of 'male' and 'female' characteristics (such as depth of emotion and loving, caring, nurturing attitudes, as opposed to and balanced by fierce hunting, fighting, or creative drive). Any of this, and much more, is belief in Duality of Deity.

Acknowledging the 8 Sabbats; Celebrating the Wheel of the Year

This is concerned with nature observance, working in and observing cycles through nature and mirrored in our own lives, and includes moon cycle ceremonies. This observance and attunement is important for the proper understanding of a particularly prominent theme in Wiccan practice – that of Life, Death, and Rebirth. Celebrating the Sabbats, along with the Esbats (full moon ceremonies) and the moon's cycle in general, either alone or as part of a group, is a major part of Wiccan practice.

The Use of Ritual and Ritual Tools

Casting a formal circle; using tools such as an athame, a wand, a pentacle, and a chalice; or invoking deity to your work; are all tenets of Wiccan practice. These tools and formalised rituals are not always necessary though. For example, a Wiccan can just as easily cast a protective circle mentally with no fuss or tools, if needed. This usually comes after quite a bit of practice in the more formal setting, though. The purpose of ritual is to distract the conscious mind and let the subconscious take over, and a practiced and well-known ritual will serve this purpose admirably.

Belief and Adherence to the Wiccan Laws

Two main laws define Wicca: Threefold Return and the Rede. The Law of the Threefold Return states that everything you send out comes back to you three times as strong. Some Wiccans vary on this, thinking it returns twice or 10 times as strong, for good or ill, but the general consensus is that everything you do will come back to you – in other words, cause and effect, action causing reaction.

Various versions of the Wiccan Rede are available. The one that is in the Book of Shadows I received states "Eight Words the Wiccan Rede Fulfil: An it Harm None, Do What you Will". Quite a few modern Wiccans, sadly, have no idea that this Rede is based on extracts from Aleister Crowley's *Liber AL vel Legis,* or Book of the Law, the holy book of Thelema, which says: "Do what thou wilt shall be the whole of the Law", and "Love is the Law, Love under Will".

There are also a lot of interpretations of the Wiccan Rede. The generally held one is that it means to do your best not to harm anybody or thing, or the planet, while still being true to yourself, your True Will, and looking after your own. It is very generalised moral code, and I have seen it interpreted as widely as 'Oh, I am harming micro-organisms every time I breathe. I am bad Wiccan for breaking the Rede' (yes, unfortunately there are people who take everything they read this literally), to 'Swing your fists!! (just be aware of other people's noses)'. The latter would probably be closer to my own personal leanings on the subject.

The Rede and the Law of Threefold Return are pretty much the only 'laws' that Wicca holds as any sort of standard. Your ethical and moral code is really up to you at the end of the day; personal responsibility is also a huge part of Wiccan belief.

A Formal Initiation or Degree System

This is a much-contested point from those who prefer to work alone, through need or circumstance, as opposed to coven or group working. I am including self-initiation here and working through your own levels and attainments. In a religion where there is no separate clergy, because we can each contact our own deity personally and not have to rely on a mediator, having a formal degree system (there are three degrees in Gardnerian and Alexandrian Wicca, the third and final inferring High Priest or High Priestess status) gives a loose structure and recognition to those who have worked hard and fought long for their goals and achievements. It does not make a third degree High Priest automatically superior to a first degree.

The degrees are given in recognition of work done and skills attained, and are not a permission slip to lord it over everyone else. Even in a coven situation, the leaders are just as likely to learn from the newcomers as vice versa. We never stop learning - if we stop growing, we stagnate. High

Priestess or High Priest status can be given to or acknowledged in the elders of a community who, though they may never have worked or trained in the Gardnerian-based degree system, have nevertheless achieved much through training and working within the community, and perhaps running their own groups. But in the context of Wicca it means (or should at least ideally mean) that those holding those titles have achieved a certain level of training, experience, and knowledge, which should be fairly standardised and similar throughout different covens and traditions.

Working in a Coven Situation

I am putting this in as part of the criteria of being Wiccan because the reality is that when the Book of Shadows and the rituals were created by Gardner and Valiente – and later elaborated on by Alex and Maxine Sanders, or Janet and Stewart Farrar – they were conceived of and worked as group ritual. I do not in any way mean that a person who follows the tenets of Wicca in all other ways, but for personal or circumstantial reasons chooses not to work in a coven, is in any way less of a Wiccan than a person who has a group down the road and works with them twice a month.

What I do mean is that the traditional Wiccan rituals used are just not going to have the same meaning unless they have been experienced at least once in the situation they were designed for. Take the 'Charge of the Goddess', for example. This is the prose and poetry learned by heart by each Wiccan Priestess, to repeat or elaborate upon, when she is filled with the energy of the Goddess. It is a voice and a space through which the Goddess may speak. This, when read from a book, or even memorised and recited alone, is a beautiful piece of poetical prose, undoubtedly moving and stirring. But the experience of the Goddess being called down (termed 'Drawing Down the Moon') into an adept Priestess, by her Priest, in front of the whole coven, and hearing/feeling/seeing her actually channeling the Goddess force, is something completely different. This rite is in itself a central part of Wiccan belief. Most Wiccans hold that deity is a source of power and aid, and that we are so intrinsically linked that we can channel their energy through ourselves.

'Drawing Down the Moon' is a fundamental expression and practice of this. In today's world, many who wish to work in a group cannot, as there are many more applicants than there are places in established working covens or groups. Nevertheless, for traditional Wicca, coven working is the ideal situation.

So, that is Wicca, in its most basic form. It is not the same as Witchcraft. Wiccans don't necessarily use magic. That being said, most will at least believe that magic is possible; that it is possible to effect the world by channeling and directing energy, even if they choose not to do so.

What Makes a Pagan?

What of Paganism then, what does it mean and what does it entail? It is soon told...

You may have heard it said that all Witches are Pagan, but not all Pagans are Witches. This is just not true. It makes the presumption that a Witch is the same thing as a Wiccan and, indeed, originates from a time when such was mostly true.

The second part certainly is true: not all Pagans are Witches, as Paganism when thought of as a religion or a spirituality is an umbrella term which can and does encompass many different types and strands, from Hellenists to Odinists, Druids to Wiccans. Again, not all of these strands may call themselves Pagan, but most seem to. It is so hard to generalise within the Pagan community. There will always be one or two who read this and say, 'Hey, I am a Druid/Odinist/Hellenist and I'm not a Pagan!' but you can't please all of the people all the time. A person of a Pagan persuasion could be recognised by being seen to follow these main points... generally speaking!

Belief in Multiple Gods, Rather than One

Relationship with deity is a very personal concept, but generally, Pagans see at least a Goddess or 'Mother Earth' figure as a force to be reckoned with, and usually believe in multiple Gods - polytheism. There are no go-betweens in Paganism; relationship with deity is a personal one. Pagans must figure out for themselves what deity or the God force means to them, and how to work with it. So if they make mistakes there is no absolution from the Priesthood, they pay for them and learn not to do it again. This tends to make most Pagan types quite careful in their actions, theoretically at least! Most stay aware of how they are affecting the world around them and what is happening to other beings in it.

Reverence for Nature

They see this world, all its creatures, and everything in the Universe as made of the same stuff as the Gods; therefore, it and we are holy and sacred. The human body and soul are connected with all life, not separate from, or in any way above, this planet and its creatures.

Personal Responsibility; Their Own Set of Ethics and Morals

As I said, there are no go-betweens. There is no authority body to tell a Pagan what is right or what is wrong for them to be doing (if somebody tried I have no doubt they would be told, maybe less than politely, where to get off!). All choices have consequences and must be lived with. Though they tend to make up their own rules of behavior, generally society (or non-automatically judgmental society, at least) could find very little fault with these self-imposed ethical codes and morals.

But that's Pagans. Not all Witches are Pagans. I would go so far as to say that most modern European Witches are Pagan, or follow some if not all of the Wiccan tenets. But not all of them, by any means. The fact that Witchcraft may not be Pagan or Wiccan in belief does not mean that Witches are evil or bad in some way. One of the main reasons most people have for linking Witchcraft (the use of magic in its most basic form) to Paganism and Wicca is the ability to quote those religious beliefs and Wiccan moral codes and say in the same breath, 'I'm a Witch, but we don't harm anyone'.

Witches have their own standards; even the non-religious ones have very high ethical codes in most cases. I am quite sure there are also some who don't; no group of people is without its bad apples, which is an unfortunate fact of life. Just as (I hope) we wouldn't judge every member of any community by the wrong actions of one or a few - you would NEVER do that, would you? Because it's very wrong - we can't tar all Witches with the same brush if we happen across the few who use magic for thoroughly selfish or ruthless ends, with no regard for the consequences. It would be true to say that 'all Wiccans are Pagan but not all Pagans are Wiccan' certainly. But Wiccans and Pagans can be quite different to any number of folk who simply call themselves Witches.

What then, is an Irish Witch?

I have mentioned one term for the word Witch, which is a female user of magic: *Bean Draoí* (pron. Ban-Dree). *Witch* is an Anglo-Saxon word. Its exact original meaning or etymology is much debated and argued over by modern scholars. The most generally accepted origins are that of the word Witch meaning 'to bend' or 'to know'. As the Anglo-Saxons have traditionally done our heritage and culture so much damage, using a term from their language to describe my own calling and beliefs is a bit odd. Why do I, and so many other modern Irish, adopt the word Witch as opposed to an Irish word or title to describe what we are and what we do?

I am aware of the historical connotations attached to the word, as well as the modern ones. A lot of terminology has been reclaimed from the Witch trials period, the 'Burning Times', and would not be terminology that users of magic in those days would ever have used themselves! In trying to find modern terminology that fits, it is difficult to pick just one Irish word that says it all and is widely understood. So Witch it is, for me, for now.

I do use a lot of Irish language terms and words throughout this book, and a lot of you who read this book won't have a clue how to pronounce these words and terms. They will appear in italics. I feel that it is important, if you are in any way serious about our culture and heritage, to make the effort to learn at least some of the Irish language.

Yes, I know it can be difficult to learn a new language, especially if you've only ever spoken or heard the English language. But if you want to work with Irish deity, Irish symbolism, Irish entities, Irish ancestors, or even the Irish landscape, you really do need to have at least an approximation of the Irish language. It'd be rude not to like.

Gaeilge (pron. Gayl-geh), the Irish language itself (please don't call it Gaelic!), is intrinsic to the Irish culture, to the feel of being Irish. Any language in itself reflects and revitalises the culture of those who speak it. As Alexei Kondratiev puts it, in his book, Celtic Rituals: "It is the Irish language which defines the continuity of Irish identity".

To this end, I have included, after every new Irish word or phrase, my take on a phonetic pronunciation guide. So you will see the Irish word [for example, *Bean* (meaning woman)], and then straight after it in parentheses the pronunciation guide [for example, (pron. Ban)]. Just ignore the [pron.], which is short for pronunciation, and sound out what you read in the rest of the brackets. Not all of them are that simple, but it is truly worth the effort, as it saves you from sounding rather silly to anybody who is actually familiar with the language. In this example you might have ended up calling yourself or the woman in your life a bean, as in the baked variety, instead of using the correct pronunciation of 'Ban' – quite an important distinction, for those of us not wanting to be referred to as legumes.

When thinking about titles and descriptions for spiritual or magical roles in Irish, the main problem we face lies in the quantity and complexity of the words that describe Witches and their function in Irish society. There are just so many of them!

Among them are:

- *Bandraoi* (pron. Ban-Dree): A term for a Druidess, this is what is given as the dictionary definition, but literally translated it is the same as *Bean Draoi* (woman, magic), which is a female User of Magic.
- *Bandraíodóir* (pron. Ban-Dree-o-THore): Given as 'Enchantress' in the

dictionary. *Draíodóir* (pron. Dree-o-THore) is usually a male term, meaning wizard, User/Weaver of Magic, or Enchanter. It can also be a trickster, a diviner, a sly cunning person, or a hypocrite.

- *Cailleach* (pron. Kyle-yoch): Witch in its basic form, but usually understood as the evil hag type. Given as 'witch, hag' in most dictionaries. Interestingly enough, the Collins Pocket Irish Dictionary also lists *Cailleach Feasa* (pron. Kyle-yoch Fassa) under this entry and gives the meaning as a 'fortune teller'.

- *Bansagart* (pron. Ban-sohgurth): Priestess; *Ard Bhansagart* (pron. Ard Van-Sohgurt) would be High Priestess. I am not personally too comfortable with this one. This is due to my associations with *sagart* (which is the male form, a priest) from growing up with the catholic priests. They were always *an sagart*, so the connection is strong. *Bansagart* is not a term I will be taking on board myself, but obviously is a useful one for those without the associations.

- *Banoide* (pron. Ban-idjah): Lady Teacher, or tutoress.

- *Banchosantóir* (pron. Ban-cosanthore) is a protectress.

- *Banlaoch* (pron. Ban-Layoch) is a female warrior or heroine. These all fit into elements of a priestess role, but are not complete enough on their own.

- *Banchuire* (pron. Ban-quiee-eh): A band or group of women together; *Bandáil* (pron. Ban-THawl) is a company or assembly of women.

- *Banfhile* (pron. Ban-illeh): A poetess; *Dán Diaga* (pron. THawn Thee-ahga) is sacred poetry; *Dán Ceoil* (pron. THawn key-ole) is the art of music; and *Dán* (pron. THawn) itself means a gift or offering, craft or calling, art or faculty, lot or fate. Or, a poem.

- *Cailleach Feasa* (pron. Kyle-yoch Fassa): Given in most places, as mentioned previously, as a 'fortune teller'. Its more correct or literal meaning would be 'knowledgeable Witch'; *feasa* (pron. fassa) or *fios* (pron. fiss) meaning knowledge or information. *Cailleach feasa* is also given as 'wise woman', which is more in tune with its literal meaning, while keeping its common usage in mind.

- Cailleach *Phiseogach* (pron. Kyle-yoch Feesh-ohgock): Sorceress or charm-worker. A *Piseog* (pron. Peesh-ohg) is often a family charm that's been passed. Its literal meaning is charm or spell, or superstitious practice, or superstition. Another word for a charm, spell, or amulet is *Briocht* (pron. Breeh-ochth).

- *Banfháidh* (pron. Ban-aw-eh): Prophetess; *Cailleach Fáidh* (pron. Kyle-yoch Fawh) is a 'seer Witch' and *Fáidhbhean* (pron. Fawh-Van) or *Fáidhmhná* (pron. Fawh-vNaw) are terms for women who see things 'supernaturally'. *Fáidheadoireacht* (pron. Fawh-ah-dore-ockth) is prophecy or prediction.

Any term here that starts with the prefix 'Ban-' can be adapted for male usage by removing *Ban* from the beginning of the word. So, for example, whereas *Banoide* is a female tutoress, *Oide* is a male tutor. If there is an 'h' in the word after *Ban*, it should also be removed, as this is a grammatical change. *Banchosantóir* becomes simply *Cosantóir* for a male protector or guardian.

Another major problem I have encountered is that when I do use Irish terms, not many folks actually know what they mean, and fewer still understand them in context to how they are used. Irish is such a free-flowing language when conversed in regularly that speakers have a marked tendency to let the oral usage and context of their conversation show what they mean, along with their expression and body language, as opposed to the standardised or formal definitions of each word. Words from a dictionary or *Foclóir* (pron. Fuk-lore) are not the whole picture. And even at that, some dictionaries are far more comprehensive than others!

So, what are you?

What descriptions, definitions, or 'titles' do you feel you have discovered on your path, or what means something to your deepest self? I believe that before you discard a label or a term to describe yourself, or indeed take one on, you should first understand what it means. Know your options.

Does it matter what you call yourself, how you are labelled or perceived by the outside world? Essentially, no, of course it does not. It will not (or should not) change how you feel, how you believe, or how you practice. But it helps, especially when you are starting out on a new path - or a new fork in your old path - to have it clear in your own head what your goals and options are, so you can make the best choices for yourself.

As you are reading this book, the words Irish and Witch probably interest you – maybe they even resonate with what you feel you are or want to be. Your heart may be pulling you in this direction, regardless of where in the world you are or what sort of life you are coming from. And this book is about your heart, figuring out what is really going on, what the real history is, and being true to how you want to work with that.

Being Irish

While we are dancing around the subject of being Irish and where people come from, I have noticed a lot of snobbery concerning ancestry roots. I would very much like to clear this up right from the start. Genuine Irish family ancestry does not make you Irish. By this I mean tracing your family tree or genealogy back to ancient Ireland. Due to the scattered and scarce written records available, these traces are not only highly unreliable at best, but, at worst, open to much manipulation – how many of those who have found an O'Brien somewhere along the way now claim to be direct descendants of Brian Boru? And say you do get it done with some degree of reliability. Say you do a genetic test, completely disregarding the fact that you've now given a private capitalist company rights over not only your DNA, but also that of your immediate families. Also disregarding that real scientists say that those tests are, at best, a 'genetic lottery' when it comes to the results, ie. not reliable. Say you disregard all of that, and find out you have '60% Irish DNA'...

If your great-great-great-granny came across the waters on a famine ship, surviving all odds to land your genetic make-up on foreign soil, and you are the end result of that migration, it certainly does not make you more Irish than somebody who may not have Irish blood in their veins - but has lived in or often visited this land, has taken time to observe the culture, learn the language (or at least try!), and gotten to know the people, culture, heritage and their peculiarities aplenty.

I have come across folks online time and again who type in 'I'm Irish too' when they read where I'm from. Proclaiming the words 'I am Irish', to me, means you are currently living in Ireland for a significant amount of time, or have at least spent a good part of your life - preferably through your formative years, but not necessarily - actually living in this land. Irish is an ethnicity.

It infuriates me at times, I must admit, when folks who know nothing of our culture or our land spout about being Irish, and when questioned why or how they feel this is true, they say things such as, 'Well, I am 1/16th Irish on my father's side, and I love the colour green' and that's pretty much the extent of their knowledge. And of course... green beer on Saint Patty's Day (please don't say Patty, never say Patty!). Though it is fascinating to me, the draw that being Irish or anything Celtic has to so many people through the world, I would prefer it if more was understood about us than our supposed colour preferences!

I really can't stress the following enough. It is the basis of any true understanding of Irish Witchcraft that you are likely to gain. If you want to explore your Irish roots, don't just research your family tree, don't just profess a love for anything Irish, don't just wave your tri-colour flag about on Paddy's Day.

You need to come to Ireland, if at all possible for you. A connection to this land is just that: the actuality of literally setting foot here, feeling its power rise through your body. Saying that, please don't panic if you don't feel the magic as soon as you set foot on the tarmac at the airport in Shannon or Dublin! Give yourself some time to breathe the air (avoiding initial jet engine fumes if possible), visit the special and sacred places, and imbibe the unique atmosphere of the fair isle.

Not every person reading this book will be in a position to drop everything and hop on a flight on the Emerald Isle, I do understand that. But for those who are able through physical and fiscal circumstance, and are serious about following this path - personal experiences with our culture are vital to the full picture. The experience of a visit or a stay in Ireland is unique. The people have a very laid-back outlook, and that's not just the bus drivers. We pick it up from all around us; there's an underlying relaxed attitude, a surety of purpose, that anybody who is magically aware can pick up in the right situations. Again, don't be disheartened if you only get the usual hustle and bustle while visiting Cork or Limerick cities – though it can be apparent even there if you meet the right people. Take a trip instead outside the bounds; visit the villages and towns, the pubs, the ancient sites, the local bed-and-breakfasts. A friend of ours once even commented on the kicked back and rather surprising honesty of Irish estate agents.

Arra, here's me going on with the same rose-coloured view that so many of our diaspora have. And I still live here. I always have and, I hope, always will.

Because I am in love with Ireland: the land, the people, the magic of this place. For all its faults and flaws I don't imagine I could ever be happy living anywhere else. As frustrating as they can be when dealing with the outside world, the stereotypes we see and hear about the Irish are in fact grounded in truth and stem from observations of the Irish and our way of life.

Time and again folks who come here to visit me from Britain and the United States will say that things move slower here, people are friendlier, the pace of life is more relaxed. You need to experience that to truly understand it. To be spoken to warmly in a pub, to have a local go out of her way to help get you where you need to go, or to see with your own eyes how Irish people genuinely do move at a calmer pace than in other countries, is to experience some of what Ireland is. The key is to keep expectations realistic, not to think that dancing at crossroads and the rugged Aran Islands lifestyle are what every person in Ireland does every day.

Being Irish is about just that; being in Ireland, feeling a love and a longing for Irish soil and Irish culture, connecting with Ireland. And the Witch part can apply to anybody who is using the magic that surrounds us all.

The language is of vital importance too, as mentioned previously, especially for those who can't actually live here, but even for those who do. In Ireland, we have the advantage of *Gaeilge* (pron. Gayl-gah), the Irish language, being a compulsory subject from the very start in our school system. We have *Gaelscoileanna* (pron. Gayl-skull-ennah), which are local initiative community schools that teach through Gaeilge, so every subject is learned with the Irish language as the 'mother tongue'. It is the first language while the kids are in school. The curriculum in your average Irish secondary school has a long way to go before it will hold the interest of the majority of Irish teenagers, but such facilities as the *Gaelscoileanna* will, we hope, continue to keep our language alive and vibrant today. The language won't be a chore; it will be a natural way of thinking. In our national exams, and for jobs such as county councils and similar, extra marks, points, and grades have been received for doing tests and interviews *as Gaeilge*, 'in Irish'. So there is incentive to keep the fluency rate high even after we leave school. *Gaeilge* will be second, or even first, nature to the children who attend a primary *Gaelscoil* (pron. Gayl-skull), which is the singular term for an all-Irish-speaking school, with their fluency opening the way for much further development and use of our language. As certain concepts and ideas from our history and heritage lose much in translation, a deeper understanding and use of *Gaeilge* will ensure these concepts are not lost for future generations.

We are often told that the youth of Ireland are disillusioned and disgusted with their own heritage, that they are disinterested in keeping our culture alive and growing. I can understand that – hey, I was a youth of Ireland, I have done the disinterest and rebellious stuff. It wasn't too long ago either (or wasn't, when I was first writing this book!); I still remember it rather clearly. The thing is, as we grow older, and perhaps we like to think of ourselves as wiser, things get clearer. We begin to understand more of our place in the world. Surely it's not just Irish teenagers who rebel against anything seen as old or connected to the past. Teenagers generally feel, and rightly so, that they are the future, the new generation, so why on earth would we expect them to be passionately interested in the past? This is generally speaking again, of course, and there are exceptions to every rule. I know plenty of teenagers who are wise beyond their years and thoroughly fascinated with heritage and culture and languages. It is more often though, only as our horizons broaden through experience of the wider world, that we begin to understand our place in it, to feel our roots and our grounding influences.

We start to reexamine what we previously perceived as 'old-fashioned' and not worthy of our time, and realise that perhaps these things have been around for so bloody long because they are actually worthwhile? Worth keeping and worth nurturing.

This Book

There are many books about Ireland currently available. Not all of them are written by Irish people. There are a few books that cover similar topics to those in this book. Even fewer of them are written by Irish people. This book is written by an Irish Witch. It gives information on Irish Witchcraft. To my knowledge, it is the first of its kind, from that respect. When I started to write it, I was determined to avoid the usual hand-holding we see in so many New Age books. I credit you, Dear Reader, from the outset, with integrity and with the willingness to work as hard as it takes for your knowledge. I credit you with not needing me to hold your hand every step of the way. I place the responsibility for your own development squarely on your shoulders.

This is part of the reason why you will find no prescribed rituals in this book. Throughout, I will suggest and explore themes or elements upon which to base your rituals or celebrations. These elements will come from what we have examined in Irish culture or tradition. I will not be writing the actual words for you to use. It doesn't make for an easy time of it for you, Dear Reader, but nobody ever said this was going to be easy.

With all my ritual I look the basics, figure out what the really important parts are in each one, and ad lib around that: I make it up on the spot. (Hey, at least I admit it!) Sometimes I feel moved to say certain words, or a piece will come out of me that I have no knowledge of, consciously, at least. I always go with that, but freely allowing instinct to take over in this way only really comes with confidence and practice. If you feel a bit silly or self-conscious at first, don't worry about it. You are doing the most important thing – covering the basics honestly – and the rest comes from your heart. Or, you know, channeled through you from the Otherworld, because that's a thing that happens too. In a group setting, giving each person a set role or function in the rite but leaving it up to themselves (or the spirit of the time) what words are actually used is incredibly effective. The same goes for working alone.

That way everybody knows what they are meant to be doing, and where they are meant to be, but there's no playing around with bits of paper and no mumbled or forgotten lines. Each person simply says what is in their heart. Of course, if you wish to write lines to use, that's totally up to you. I recommend learning them instead of reading them. You wouldn't walk onto a stage with your script in your hand would you? Not quite the same thing of course, but a ritual is supposed to be a bit dramatic, so, similar at least. Again, though, it is up to you. I, however, am not going to write the actual lines for you to use. They should, whether pre-prepared or spontaneous, be your words, your feelings, your heart. Not mine.

No matter how many times an author says, 'The following words/rituals/spells are just a suggestion/example, feel free to/you should change the words to suit yourself/ your circumstances', there are those who never do. They read it straight from the book with no feeling or intent, beyond nervousness that they aren't going to get it right. Then they wonder why it doesn't bring about the profound life-altering changes they were expecting. I have no intention of giving those people the opportunity. I have no desire to receive emails somewhere down the line that open with 'Your *Samhain* ritual didn't cleanse my house properly…'. If you want to do this Irish Witchcraft thing, you will have to do the work yourself. This may disappoint some of you, especially if you are looking for this book to be a 'how to be an Irish Witch' step by step guide. It's not. But it is a helping hand, a step in the right direction, a starting point or signpost, for those who are willing to put the effort into their own development.

All rites or rituals should start with the creation/recognition of a sacred space, in whatever way is usually used. Anything from a formal 'casting the circle', to an invitation to the Gods, Guides, and Guardians to attend, to a simple declaration that the space which has been set aside is suitable. You are trying to do as it says: create a sacred space. Make it different from the usual space. Open a bridging point between the worlds. Do it in whatever way you feel comfortable. Then follow the elements or themes contained in each particular rite, which you can use to compose your own ceremonies or celebrations. Afterwards, don't forget to shut it down and clear up your mess, both physical and energetic!

So, if you are genuinely interested in Ireland, learn the language. No groaning at the back there, it is important! Visit Ireland. Live here if possible. And if you are still genuinely interested in Irish Witchcraft, learn the history. Feel the magic.

I hope this book will give you some useful starting points.

I

How It Was

1

Myth and Legends

My initial endeavor in this chapter was to be the extraction of examples of magic in our myth. Sounds interesting, doesn't it? The reason I put in a whole chapter about this is that magic and its use is central to what our modern perception of a Witch actually is, and we can see examples of this use of magic through our myths. My biggest problem and one that I hit upon quite overwhelmingly from the very beginning of this endeavor has been that of 'where on earth to start?' Magic is so intrinsically linked through all the myths, all the legends, all the great sagas and stories of our country – there can be no separation, no siphoning out of specific examples to prove this point or that. The magic is in everything that our people have ever done – or in all that has been written down, at the very least.

An Cailleach

The Witch, *An Cailleach* (pron. On Kyle-yock, have you forgotten already?!), appears through many of the myths and legends. The usual place for a person by the title of Witch or *Cailleach* is as the hag or the troublemaker. *Fionn Mac Cumhaill* (pron. Fee-yun Mah Kool) met the daughters of a fairy king at the caves of Cesh Corran, four hags as hideous and terrible as any man's imagination ever conceived of. The Witches got the better not just of him, but of his band of warriors, *Na Fianna* (pron. Fee-anna). They all ended up bound tight in the caves, all but one: Goll Mac Morna. He kept his wits about him, bested these Witches, and freed the warriors. All four sisters were killed. In this, we see the all-too-familiar example of the Witch as evil female power, bested by the men.

There were 'cult' *Caillaighe* (Witches) though, such as the *Cailleach Bhéara*, or 'hag of Beara', who lived on the Beara peninsula in the county of Cork, in the southwest of Ireland. Indeed, she is known from the southern tip of Cork to the North of Scotland, in various forms and guises. That knowledge of her was so far-reaching may be explained by the report that she was tremendously long lived. Proinsias MacCana quotes from 'an early note' that: "she entered upon seven periods of youth, so that every husband used to pass from her to death through old age, and so that her grandchildren and great-grandchildren were peoples and races". This is no ordinary neighbourhood hag, rather she seems to be a folk memory of an ancestral spirit, shaper, and guardian of the land, or even a Goddess.

The Otherworld

Magic itself, and the use of magic is predominant in practically all of our myths and legends. Everybody's doing it, and those who aren't doing it themselves are looking for people who do it, to aid them in some way. The rest are, at the very least, influenced by it.

When writing about digging around in the folklore department of University College, Dublin, one of our foremost Irish language poets Nuala Ni Dhomhnaill writes:

> [T]here is a drawer in the index entitled 'Neacha neamhbeo agus nithe nach bhfuil ann' ('Unalive beings and things that don't exist'). Now I am not the greatest empiricist in the world but this one has even me stumped. Either they exist or they don't exist. But if they don't exist why does the card index about them stretch the length of my arm?
> From the New York Times Book Review, January 8, 1995.

These are references in both folklore and mythology to the Otherworld, *An Saol Eile* (pron. On Sail Ella). It literally means, in modern translation, 'the other life'. As with most things in our language, the phrase carries more meaning than is conveyed through its literal translation. The use of the term *an saol eile* rather than *an domhan eile* for the Otherworld (*domhan* being the noun for 'the world' itself) has always struck me as interesting. Using *Saol* is usually more about perception than physicality – *An saol mór* is 'the whole world', and *Sin an saol (agat)* means 'such is life' or 'such is the life you have'. It is not so much the actuality or geography of a person's existence, but more their perceptions, their situation, and their making sense of their senses.

Slipping easily from one world to the Other is normal through our myths and stories. Some of the more fantastical descriptions can be seen as 'otherworldly' or 'supernatural' by us now. To the people involved, and to the people hearing the tales, they were completely natural. The dead walked among us, fantastic beasts and feats were not so fantastic when you considered them as simple crossing over of strength, powers or imagery *as an saol eile*, 'out of the Otherworld'. As Nuala so concisely puts it in that same New York Times article:

> *Even the dogs in the street in West Kerry know that the 'otherworld' exists, and that to be in and out of it constantly is the most natural thing in the world.*

The *Seanchaí* (pron. Shan-a-key), or 'storyteller', would maybe describe *An Saol Eile* as a place that is like ours, but not quite. Everything that's here is there, but the things there are a bit brighter, a bit better, a bit more fabulous or intense than those here. The sun is more golden and the moon is more silver there, the fruits more ripe and ready, and the flowers more delightful.

The general term of the Otherworld actually covers many different realms. In modern terms, you might see it as similar to the 'astral plane' – where each thing has a counterpart, and to manoeuvre or effect change there can cause corresponding changes here. It is also a place in its own right, populated by weird and wonderful beings, which one can meet and greet and even fight in certain states of walking between the worlds.

There are other realms that form a part of *An Saol Eile*, such as the more traditional realm of the Underworld, or land of the dead, ruled by Donn, lord of death. There are many different places and landscapes contained in the one idea of the Otherworld, places sometimes seen in myths, such as in 'The Voyage of Bran', as islands to be visited. They are accessed variously: over the sea as islands, or through a *Sidhe* (pron. Shee), which originally may have meant an 'abode' but came to mean the magical passage graves, tumuli, ring forts, or any of the other surviving ancient earthworks or monuments or mounds. It could also be accessed through pools or lakes, under which the Otherworld entrances were said to be; natural caves or mountaintops; or through the magical mists that descended and caused folks to become disoriented or lost. We see lands such as *Eamhain Abhlach*, the 'sacred place of apples'; *Tir inna mBeo*, or the 'Land of the Living', where none know sickness or ill health and all have an innocence that leaves the pleasure of love and passion unsullied by any form of guilt; *Magh Meall*, which means something like 'plain of joy', where the ladies are numerous and always pleasing to the eye and the soul, apparently - a land filled with wonderful music from birds and instruments unseen, inexhaustible vessels of plenty to rival the Dagda's own cauldron, and much food and drink of delightful variety and taste; and of course the wonderful *Tir na nÓg*, 'Land of the Young', to which Fionn Mac Cumhaill's (pron. Fee-yun Mah Kool) son *Oisín* (pron. Ush-een) was led by *Niamh* (pron. Nee-av) of the Golden Hair.

Users of Magic

With such a blending of the mythical and the real, and the hopping in and out of such fascinating places, how can one hope to separate out who or what is most important from our ancient past? The Tuatha Dé Danann, or 'People/Tribe of Danú', are those who come to our own public notice most often, and, as modern Witches and seekers of Irish magic, they are the ones who will be most useful to us in our own paths. We should, at the very least, be familiar with that Godly tribe in their most honest forms and functions.

When I say 'most useful to us', in that I 'use' a God or Goddess, I certainly do not mean using in the sense of selfish gain at the expense of others. It is more like a contractual relationship: mutual and respectful give-and-take. Having a working knowledge of the Gods of this land is essential for any sort of respectful interaction. Further on, you will hear me talk about my 'Gods, Guides, and Guardians'. It is only polite of me to introduce some of them to you now.

But don't just take my word for it and go no further. Look up the books and websites recommended in the bibliography and resources section, immerse yourself in the legends, lap up the language in its most honest and sympathetic translations. What I offer is only an abbreviated form of the rich tapestry of stories and tales, symbolism and attributes that the Tuatha Dé Danann, and indeed any of our mythical or legendary figures, have to offer. But for now, I hope it will suffice to interest, excite, and inform you, Dear Reader.

The Dagda

> Modern Functions: God of abundance, fertility, and male sexuality and prowess – the great provider. A God of agriculture and the sun. Genuine mirth and confidence are held by him, and care for his people as a wise father would care for his family/children. Physical strength and power. Husband of the Mórrígan, has a child with Bóann.

Chief God of the Irish. There are many tales of his prowess, his appetites (both sexual and culinary), and his tremendous size and strength. Dagda means 'the Good God', but he holds many titles and jobs within the ranks of the Irish deities. As *Eochaidh Ollathair* (pron. Uh-key Ull-aher), which means 'Eochaidh the Great Father', and *Aedh Ruadh Ró-fhessa* (pron. A-ah Roo-ah Roe-Essa), which means 'red fire of all knowledge', it is told he holds much wisdom, and he is proclaimed to be the - or at least a - God of Druidism. He is described as having perfected the 'heathen science' – that is, the magic and knowledge of Druidic lore, as judged by later scholar and scribes.

His strength is emphasised in his appearance: he is said to be a very big and tall man, with remarkable eyes, thighs, and shoulders and a fine gray cloak about him. He has elsewhere been portrayed as a peasant and as an 'ugly brute'. His countenance is 'broader than half a plain'. Indeed, he cleared 12 plains and cut the paths of 12 rivers, each in one night, and he controls the weather and the crops for the Tuatha Dé Danann. He was master of the natural environment.

He carries a club of such power that he could kill with ease using one end of it, the rough end – and bring the dead back to life just as easily by switching to the other end, which is smooth. This twofold power of life and death is the mark of a great magician – again, a power that can walk between both worlds. He is also marked by a tremendous size in all things he does and carries. In the second Battle of *Magh Tuireadh* (known as Moytura) it is told that the same iron club is so large and heavy that it marks a great furrow in the ground as he trails it along behind him, as deep as the boundary ditch between two provinces, and his blows sweep down whole ranks of the Fomorian or *Fomhóraigh* (pron. Foe-vore-ah, and meaning 'under-spirits/demons') enemy.

When he addresses the enemy to buy time and for a little reconnaissance mission in their camp, they try to best him by using his reputation (for being a great one to eat, especially the *leite*, or porridge) against him. They fill a great hole in the ground with a porridge containing a full 80 measures of milk, with the same again of meal and fat, to which they have added whole carcasses of pigs, goats, and sheep. When they order him to eat the lot or be killed, the Dagda sets to with a genuine gusto using his own spoon or ladle, which was said to be so big 'that a man and woman (married couple) could have lain together in it'. He eats the lot, right down to the gravel-filled bottom, and then falls into a satisfied doze with a belly 'as big as a house-boiler', leaving the confounded *Fomhóraigh* to stick to their word and honour his truce; he had, after all, completed his end of the bargain. The pit in the ground was probably a mockery of the Dagda's own cauldron, the mystical cauldron of plenty. It was said that once a company or an assembly was fed from this vessel, they could never go away unsatisfied.

8

The Dagda also possessed a magical harp, with which he had full command of the 'three noble strains', which any harper should know. These are the Strain of Lament, which caused the audience to weep uncontrollably; the Strain of Laughter, which made listeners happy and merry and caused laughter; and the Strain of Slumber, which steeped all who heard its tones into a profound and deep, magical sleep. He called his harp in a strange refrain:

"Come, apple sweet murmurer, come, four angled frame of harmony, come, Summer, come, Winter, from the mouths of harps and bags and pipes".

It would fly to his hand through the air from anywhere upon hearing his call. With his proficient command of music and magic, he was powerful indeed.

His dwelling originally was at *Brúgh na Bóinne* (pron. Brew nah Boe-innya), or Newgrange, which possibly illustrates his origins as a solar deity (the passage tomb being a solar-based construction), and later as a very much alive and kicking personification of the sun and its power and strength. He held Newgrange until it was tricked from him by a clever verbal ruse of *Oenghus Óg* (pron. En-ghuss Oh-gh), or *Mac ind Óg* (pron. Mack ind Oh-gh), 'The Young Lad': his own son by the Goddess Bóann of the Boyne River. She was a Lady of fertility, and abundance; a cow Goddess (*bó* in Irish is still used to mean cow), as cattle represented the wealth and providence of a *tuath*. The Dagda needed to lay with Bóann in his role as the keeper of corn and milk; it would ensure the fertility of the land. Her representation as the river is symbolic of the free flowing milk from the herds. To conceal their tryst from her husband Elcmhaire, who had promised to return by nightfall, the Dagda caused the sun to stand still for nine full months; and so Oenghus was conceived and born and safely fostered off, all in the same day. Again we see the Dagda as a solar deity, and that Newgrange is designed around the Winter Solstice, so to my mind, the myth seems to refer to the birth of the sun's son (rebirth of the sun, as happens at the Winter Solstice).

He was one of the main participants in the preparations and fighting itself of the Battle of *Magh Tuireadh*, over which Lugh held sway. He promised to assist by shaking the mountains, draining the lakes, and bringing showers of fire. Even before the tales grew tall and muddled, as myths are wont to do, the origin of this most important battle would have involved the Dagda: "as figure bringing light into darkness and thereby resolving the conflict between sun and earth" (Ó hÓgáin). Even in its present form, the myth of *Magh Tuireadh* features him strongly and squarely placed not as the divine king, but as the protector of the people. Before the battle, on the feast of *Samhain*, he left for a meeting with the Mórrígan, his wife – after which she promised to use destructive magic to aid the Tuatha Dé Danann against the Fomhóraigh enemy. In his role as a father figure of the Gods, he must meet the Goddess of war, who will to some extent pre-define the outcomes of the battle – and physically unite with her to ensure her help and goodwill, to provide safety and victory for his people. It is possibly indicated that he is an older God from the rest of the Tuatha Dé Danann, as shown by his father role... but please note that *Ollathair* means 'Father of many', and not 'the All Father' as some would have you believe.

Danú

> *Modern Functions: Mother Goddess, magical ancestor. Goddess of Soil and irrigation. Protector of the land. Goddess of fertility and bounty. Great Queen of all, mate of the Dagda.*

A Note for the 2nd Edition:
I am leaving this section in, largely as it was first published; but subsequent years' research and experience has led me to believe that Danú is not, in fact, an Irish deity. Controversial, I know. Please do bear in mind that this is my own belief right here.

In all of my travels and Journeys across Ireland, in this world and the Other, I have not come across any entity or Being that presents as this Goddess. And I have specifically looked. Maybe she doesn't like me, doesn't want to have anything to

10

do with me, or just doesn't pay any attention to me. Any of that is possible! To be
clear, I do believe she is a Goddess, probably a river Goddess that originated with
the tribes that lived in what is now Central and Eastern Europe, around the River
Danube. I just do not believe - personally - that she is an Irish Goddess, nor that
she is interchangeable with Anú. So, take that as you will.

A progenitor of the Tuatha Dé Danann, she is the archetypal mother figure
– though we don't actually hear much about as a personality in her own
right. I'll bet that sounds familiar to any of you who are mothers out there!
Everybody knows you are there, knows who you are and what you do, but
as a person? Not so much knowledge going around. Danú (pron. D-Anoo)
is sort of like that.

She is known as the mother of many deities, indeed of a whole race of
deities, as the name Tuatha Dé Danann is most commonly translated as
'people of the Goddess Danú'. [She may be interconnected with Anú, who's
name means 'abundance', and who may be connected to the great prosperity
of the province of Munster. A fertility and land Goddess, without a doubt,
we can see to this day the two mountain tops called *Dá Chích Nanann*, which
means the 'two paps of Anú'. They lie just southeast of Kerry and do indeed
look tremendously like two great breasts sitting there in the Irish landscape
for all to see. It is interesting to note that the pronunciation of *Dá Chích
nDanann* is exactly the same as *Dá Chích Nanann*, as the D falls silent. The
pronunciation has been the same since medieval times, according to author
Dáithí Ó hÓgáin. This would make it the two paps of Danú instead of Anú.
If Anú is a later form of Danú, the name might have come from a connection
between the land's fertility and the Old Irish word *anae*, which meant wealth.
Those later scribes were a presumptuous lot at times. Anú is possibly a
Goddess of prosperity; it is she to whom Munster owes its bounty, for she
takes special care of that province.]

Danú was possibly viewed in triplicate form. Her followers were named
as *fir trí nDéa*, which means either 'men of the three Gods' or 'men of the
three Goddesses'. This may be a later development, but also may be evidence
of the Goddess in triplicate form. As ever, the ancient texts do not come

with modern instructions for interpretation, so the interpretation is open to debate.

Lugh

Modern Functions: God of light, many talented one, Divine King. Keeper of oaths and bargains. God of martial training and skill, and also of crafts and the arts.

Lugh (pron. Loo) is known as the *Ildánach* (pron. Ill-dawn-ock), which means 'possessing or skilled in many arts together'. This title comes mainly from a story in the Battle of Magh Tuireadh. Lugh showed up at Tara – the seat of the high king of Ireland and the Tuatha Dé Danann – while a great feast was in progress. The feast was in honour of the kingship being restored to Nuada. It was the tradition then that nobody without a useful skill might enter Tara, so when Lugh arrived at the door, the gatekeeper asked what skill he possessed that might gain him entry. Lugh declared himself a wright, only to be told they had one of those. He tried to get in on his skills as a blacksmith. Same thing: they already had a very good one. He listed his skills as a harper, a hero, and a champion, but of course they had the Dagda, Oghma, and quite a few others for such things. Lugh said he was also a poet, a historian, a sorcerer, a leech, a cup-bearer, a craftsman in metal, but the Tuatha Dé Danann were already well populated with such folk. It seems none of Lugh's many talents would be of any use to him there until he delivered his final question. This is paraphrased, of course, for I was not there myself that particular day. 'Tell me, Gatekeeper', said the Ildánach, 'do you have one inside the court who can do all of these things?' The gatekeeper admitted they had not, and Lugh was permitted to enter Tara.

Lugh is the grandson of Balor, the Fomhóraigh God, and king. Balor has been said to have been an original sun God - with his single bright and baleful eye that could destroy any it was turned upon in full force. His name comes from the Celtic Boleros, which in turn may have been connected to the root *bhel*, which means 'flash' (McNeill, Ó hÓgáin).

It was prophesied that the child of Balor's daughter would bring about his demise. So he had his only daughter, Eithne (pron. Eth-neh, and sometimes given as Ethlinn), locked in a tower on an island to ensure he never gained a grandchild and so lose his life. A Tuatha Dé Danann warrior, Cian (Pron. Kee-an), gained access to the tower with the help of a Witch. He dressed as a woman, for only women were permitted near Eithne. They fell in love (or at least in lust, as he didn't have long in the tower, after all), and she grew large with child, through the magically aided and improbable union of the two warring races. It is sometimes written that she had triplets and only one son survived. The son was Lugh, and the inevitable order came for him to be killed. But the soldiers took pity on him and put him to sea in a basket from the base of the tower instead, so that he may have some chance of further survival. He was found and subsequently fostered first by Manannán Mac Lir, and by Tailtiu (pron. Toll-chew, with the 'toll' as in 'doll'), the queen of the Firbolg. The Firbolg were another not-so-friendly race, and so Lugh contained and somewhat represented the interests of, the trinity of the main races in Ireland at the time.

He later started the Tailteann games, held on the harvest festival Lúnasa or Lughnasadh (pron. Loo-Nassah) - feats of daring and grace, battles of wit and wisdom, games of strategy and skill - in honour of his foster mother, Tailtiu. They came to be held at what is now Teltown in County Meath. And he did indeed go on to slay his grandfather, Balor, in a later battle, with a slingshot missile through the eye, though he also possesses a wonderful spear, one of the four treasures of the Tuatha Dé Danann. Another version of this story (much less romantic, so more likely to be close to the truth!) has Cian of the Tuatha Dé Danann and Eithne, daughter of Balor, of the Fomhóraigh, married to unite the two peoples, Lugh is born of this. The Tuatha Dé Danann were great ones for power and magic but didn't seem to be much for the day-to-day running of things, such as farming and animal husbandry, which is why they needed the Fomhóraigh skills. But the unity of the tribes didn't last long: They fought the second battle of Magh Tuireadh, and the Fomhóraigh were defeated.

As to the possible origins of the Balor/Lugh myth, the following makes sense to me. At the height of the Summer, the sun's baleful glare might have been quite capable of the destruction of crops as it turned its full force on the earth, and so the hero king, at Lúnasa, was called upon to destroy it and thus save the harvest. Balor is possibly a representation of a much earlier Bronze Age sun God.

His usual title is Lugh *Lámhfada* (pron. Lawv Fodth-ah), which means 'of the long arm' and is probably related to his method of fighting with his spear... his throw (and therefore his killing hand) extended a great way from where he stood. It may also be a reference to the length of his Otherworldly reach - controlling of the sun, moon, and stars - like the Indian God Savitar, who is known as 'of the wide hand'.

Lugh is one of the most colourful and interesting characters through the legends. His name means 'The Shining One' and he is a God of light and life, but not specifically a solar deity. It is true that when he arrived at the battle with the Fomhóraigh that they felt they beheld the rising of the sun, but it was, in fact, the light radiating from Lugh's face and head. He often appears as victor over malevolent beings from *An Saol Eile* - no doubt reminding the Irish that, no matter how close or frightening the Otherworld could seem at times, victory over the trials from there, and safety from its more menacing inhabitants, was possible. And yet he is also part of the negative side to the Otherworld, in that his Fomhóraigh mother is of the race of 'demons' who seem to symbolise the darkness. He embodies the balance, being equally at home in the depths of the passage tombs or the brilliant and dazzling light on emergence. He appears as youthful, handsome, and athletic, a true shining hero type, sometimes with a halo of light around his head.

He is perhaps one of the most highly representative personifications of a very persistent theme in Irish myth and legend: that of the Divine King. This is played out in a literal kingship - he goes on to be king of the Tuatha Dé Danann at Tara after Nuada and leads the battle against the Fomhóraigh. It is also seen that he is teamed with a Goddess/woman who represents the land and its prosperity, as Proinsias MacCana puts it in his Celtic Mythology:

When Conn 'of the Hundred Battles', the famous king of Tara, visited Lugh he found him seated in state as a king of the Otherworld and attended by a young and regally dressed woman who is identified as the sovereignty of Ireland.

This took place through a vision, or a journey to the Otherworld led or called by Lugh, which Conn had while in the presence of his Druids and poets. That the woman gave him a cup to drink signified that he was the rightful king of the time, but Lugh also went on to prophecy the long line of kings who would succeed Conn's reign.

Tailtiu, Lugh's foster mother, was also an earth Goddess. She was taken in marriage by the Firbolg king Eochaidh Mac Eirc and, as such, was made a queen of those people: she safeguarded the fertility of the land. Before her marriage, she was a daughter of the king of the 'Great Plain', or the Land of the Dead. She took care of the Divine King, in the role of a mother and possibly later his lover. The Goddess in Pagan literature is often seen as fulfilling all roles. She never dies, just goes through continual renewal and rebirth - and so can fulfill the roles of mother, sister, lover, teacher, in her many guises. Tailtiu ensured the fertilising light would strike where and when necessary for the prosperity of the land and her people.

The Cailleach Bhéara, correlated with a figure named Buí, or Boí according to Tomás Ó Cathasaigh, is said in some tales to be the wife of Lugh - her intimate connection with the land implies some links with sovereignty - and she is closely associated in this sense with the Knowth monument, which lies beside Newgrange in County Meath. The burial site of the Goddess Carmun is also traditionally associated with the festival of Lúnasa, and the Goddess buried there had such similar attributes to Tailtiu that it seems to underline Lugh's status and rightful place as the 'divine prototype of human kingship'.

Lugh is a God who presided over oaths and bargains, perhaps in his function as King, who were often called to pass judgement over matters brought before them. Although Nuada was king before him, he gladly gave up the throne for Lugh to lead the Tuatha Dé Danann into the second battle of Magh Tuireadh. He kept the kingship role after Nuada was slain in that battle. Lugh is a God of warrior prowess, martial skill, training, and talent - but also a God of arts and crafts, called upon whenever any of his specific skills are needed. He fathered the boy who is painted as a hero - Cú Chulainn - by a Milesian maiden named Dectera, and appeared through the lad's life many times as an aid, inspiration, and adviser.

Brighid

Modern Functions: Goddess of poetry, healing, and smithcraft. Protector of children, mothers, and women in childbirth.

Her name seemed to have originally meant 'the exalted one'. She's the daughter of the Dagda, and in some versions of the story had two sisters, both of whom were also named Brighid (pronounced Breedj). As three entities, they rule over *Filíocht* (pron. Fill-ee-ockt), which is poetry, along with healing and smithcraft. She is the patroness of poetry and learning, for the *Filidh* (pron. Filleh) were the contemporaries, and later the successors, of the christian-oppressed Druids in their roles of seers, teachers, advisers of rulers, witnesses of contracts. They held the power of satirical sanction (where public mockery could be made of a person for dishonourable deeds or ignoble actions), right up until the 1600s C.E. - when Irish traditional culture was 'officially' overcome by the invaders systems. Brighid held sway over those concerned with the highest matters of society; she was expert herself not just in poetry and learning in the traditional sense, but also divination and prophecy. She is described as a woman of poetry, the Goddess whom the seer-poets adored. She is also described as a noblewoman, who is multi-formed multi-faceted multi-magical and is a sort of muse figure for the Filidh, who can magically appear to a poet as he is composing.

As patroness of the smiths, she also held vast importance. The blacksmith was a person of great consequence in Irish society. Many laws and much literature survive to illustrate this, and even in rural Ireland up until not

16

so long ago, the community blacksmith held an incredibly important place, until the car and tractor brought an end to the reliance on the horse. As controller and worker of iron, smiths were seen in a community or village as vital in ensuring *Na Daoine Sidhe* didn't get it all their own way - for those magical creatures hate the touch or feel of cold iron.

In Brighid's capacity as a healer, she cared for her people - with special consideration for aiding conception, caring for child-bearing women, and helping through childbirth. She is the Goddess of hearth and home, and the tradition of bringing her indoors at Imbolg to ensure the fertility of the household is still strong in places. Her feast time is Imbolg when she holds the most strength and prominence, which has survived in the celebration of Saint Brigid's Day here on the first of February. A lot of schools and families make the solar St. Brigid's Cross every year. It is woven of rushes or grasses to bring good fortune to the house and family for the year to come.

And so we come to the interesting crossover between Brighid the Goddess and Saint Brigid who ruled her monastery in Kildare (*Cill Dara* in Irish, which means 'church of the oak' or 'the oaken wood') around 500 C.E. This goodly lady was from her birth deemed magical - she was the daughter of a Pagan Druid, and born on the threshold of the house, both in and out: a true walker between the worlds. She was suckled from the milk of a white cow with red ears, which in Irish tradition is a magical cow with strong Otherworld associations, and appears many times through the stories as almost divine in its power and attraction to those who own or see them. Her wet cloak can be hung on the rays of the sun, showing that she can gain assistance from even the sun's natural power as it bends to aid her. Another significance of harnessing the sun's power is the description that any house she abides in seems from the outside to be ablaze with light.

There are many miraculous deeds attributed to her throughout her childhood and early years, as well as her unending charity and godliness in caring for the poor and the sick. When she rules as Abbess of the monastery at Kildare there is much blending of older Pagan rites and customs, which would have been abhorrent to the Roman church. Brigid, when faced with a nun whose womb had swelled with child 'through youthful desire of pleasure', proceeded to make the fetus magically disappear so the young girl wouldn't be turned out of her convent. It isn't clear whether this was through the use of her own power or with magical or medicinal herbs, but either way, it certainly echoes the concerns and sympathies of the earlier Goddess. It also holds against everything the Roman church was taking a stance on at the time, and ever since, and certainly points to the possibility that Brigid was one of Ireland's first recorded abortion service providers. (Thankfully we have many more now, but only since we Repealed the 8th Amendment in 2018 - go look that one up!). The easy and amenable attitudes of Irish christians in general at the time is refreshing to subjects such as diversity, authority, and the role of women. They generally accepted that sexuality is a natural inclination for humans, even if they considered it an inclination we should strive to gain control of. Unfortunately, none of these more relaxed tendencies have survived in the modern catholic christian. The only remnant of such a moderate time in Irish christian history is the way in which the Irish custom of private confession came to be the norm, as opposed to the previous thought that a person's sins were the domain of the public. It was the Irish christians who originally placed the responsibility for sin on the individual's conscience rather than on how the community or church viewed or judged you – though at the time we chose to confess to those of our own *anam chairde* (soul friends) who we felt would best listen, rather than a specific clergy person.

February first is the day Brigid is recorded to have died or, rather - as Cogitosus calls her in Thomas Cahill's 'How the Irish Saved Civilisation' - Saint Brigid...

'Falling asleep, safely laid down the burden of her flesh and followed the Lamb of God into the heavenly mansions'.

I sorta like that description, actually.

There are so many holy and healing wells, place names, and sacred sites throughout the entire country dedicated to Brigid that it would be hard to discount the idea that the saint took over more or less directly in the eyes of the people from the Goddess Brighid. The ancient customs and traditions are still very strong in many Irish homes, though not commonly understood to be pertaining to the Goddess Brighid rather than to the Saint Brigid. Our national TV and radio stations, *Radio Teilifís Èirinn* (RTE), had the Brigid's cross as their symbol for a long time, and it is still to be seen in many official places throughout the Irish cultural experience. Her popularity in Ireland, it is said, is second only to Patrick. I personally question that Patrick holds the greater sway in the everyday life and practices of the Irish people rather than Brigid, or a greater place in our hearts and national identity.

Dian Cécht

Modern Functions: God of power, and a God of healing, health, and herbalism. Can be evoked when new paths of healing need to be found, as well as the strength and fortitude to travel them.

His name seems to have meant 'he who swiftly travels'. This could refer to how quickly his cures came into effect on a person, which was by all accounts rather miraculous, or how quickly he could be evoked when needed. One of the texts describes him as 'going roads of great healing', so it could also refer to breakthroughs he made (that is, the distance he had travelled with his breakthroughs). He is the divine medic of the Tuatha Dé Danann, who crafted the fabulous silver hand for Nuada, as mobile and dexterous as his real one had been when the king lost his arm. This enabled Nuada to carry on as the high king, before Lugh took over; for a king could not be any less than whole and perfect. Any physical impairment was viewed as symbolic of a blemish on the land and the people, just as any impairment of judgment or logic was.

Dian Cécht (pron. Dee-ann Kay-cht) affected his cures and medical miracles through a blend of powerful healing and magical herbs. In the Battle of Magh Tuireadh he was able to bring those who had fallen dead on the field of battle back to life. He sang incantations over a special well in which the mortally wounded were bathed, thus bringing back their life force in full. He is quoted there as saying: "Any man who is wounded will be fully healed by me unless his head be cut off, or the membrane of his brain or his spinal cord be severed".

There are many charms on record that evoke his powers; one such is for a salve, which is applied with the words: "I put my trust in the salve which Dian Cécht left with his family that whatever on which it goes be whole!". Again we see the blend of herbs and magic associated with this deity - the salve would have been prepared with a specific recipe in mind. Ireland was known to have the largest store of medical and herbal knowledge in Europe, back in the day, but much of it went unrecorded. It was stored in the heads of the practitioners, with vast medical knowledge passed through families from generation to generation.

In his capacity as 'the healing sage of Ireland' lies much of his power and wisdom. There are records of early law tracts that set the scene on many issues, through their wise judgements, and these are attributed to Dian Cécht.

Manannán Mac Lir

> *Modern Functions: A Lord of the Otherworld; a guide and a guardian of those realms. Lord of the sea and a keeper of those who journey upon it.*

Meaning 'Manannán son of Lir', Manannán Mac Lir (pron. Man-ann-AWN Mack Leer) is a very popular deity. Rather than being perceived as the sea itself, as his father is, he is the Lord of the Sea. Lir does not appear often through the legends, and when he does it is as a vast ocean presence, as tremendous as the waves, and as impersonal as the storms at sea.

Manannán escorts us over and under the sea. *Tir na nÓg* and the Land of the Dead are part of his domain; he is a gatekeeper and a guide. He is a trickster and an illusionist; he embodies the unknowable, misleading (to the unwary), and mischievous aspects of both the sea and *Na Daoine Sidhe*. He is a shifter of shape, entering our world in a myriad of different guises and forms.

Manannán is a worker of very powerful magic, controlling the weather with which the sea can aid or hamper our journey, and to this end, he is in possession of many magical objects. He wielded a sword called the Answerer – no armour could resist its cleave. He sailed in a boat called Ocean-sweeper – it travelled without oar or sail and obeyed the guiding thought of any who sailed in it. He kept a loyal steed named *Aonbarr* – a horse that could travel as fast and sure over the sea as on land. He wore a great cloak of many colours, as shimmering and mutable as the sea itself is when seen from on high. His role and function as a protector of the island of Ireland can be seen in the fact that when we were threatened it is said that the hostile invaders heard his turbulent footstep and the vigourous clapping of his cloak as they camped at night. His throne in this world may lie on the Isle of Man, named for Manannán himself, which can be seen on a clear day from the Irish coast, though very far in the distance.

Although he doesn't appear in either of the Magh Tuireadh battles, in later texts he is definitely listed in the ranks of the Tuatha Dé Danann. He leads folks to the Otherworld, ever the guide and the guardian of the gates. Just as he led Cormac Mac Airt from the king's throne at Tara to his Otherworldly realm, he may still guide us on our journey to his court.

Goibhniu

> *Modern Functions: God of protection and charms, called on to aid in protective and dispersing magic. God of craft workers, especially the modern-day blacksmith.*

Goibhniu's name (pron. Gwiv-noo) is derived from *gabha* (pron. Gow-a, the first part to rhyme with Now), which simply means Smith, and is preeminent of the triad of craft-workers for the Tuatha Dé Danann (the other two being

21

Luchtaine the wright and Creidhne the metal-worker). Goibhniu is afforded a place of high honour among the Tuatha, for when Nuada calls a year-long conference of the Dagda and Oghma before battle, he also calls for Goibhniu and Dian Cécht, 'his two kinsmen'. The blacksmith says of his own spears; "No spear-point which my hand forges will make a missing cast, no skin which it pierces will taste life after that". Goibhniu forges the heads, Luchtaine constructs the shafts, and Creidhne makes the rivets to hold the lot together.

He is known for his protective and therapeutic powers as well as his skills. A traditional Irish charm calls on him to aid in the removal of a thorn. His influence as a wielder of magic has also survived through the ages: The Lorica or Deer's Cry, attributed to St. Patrick in the 400s C.E. invokes God's strength 'against spells of witches, smiths, and wizards' – society's most dangerous users of magic. He survives to present day in folktales of *An Gobán Saor* (pron. on Gubb-awn Sayer), which means 'Gobbán the Wright', a witty master craftsman in many tales, who uses his resourcefulness to outwit his enemies.

Goibhniu is quite an important deity, aside from his talent as a smith, as he ruled over the Otherworld feast known as *Fledh Ghoibhnenn*, 'the Feast of Goibhniu'. Those who sat at his feast, and ate and drank there, were left forever apart from age and decay. The main part of the feast was an intoxicating beverage distilled from honey, that was similar to a sacred drink of the Gods in many other cultures.

Oghma

Modern Functions: Warrior and champion of the Gods, God of great strength. Weaver of words and language; patron of writers and speakers alike.

Known as *Grian-aineach*, 'of the sun-like countenance' and *Grian-éces*, which meant 'sun-poet'. He was also called *Mac Ealadh*, which means 'son of art'. As such he was: "a man most knowledgeable in speech and poetry" (Ó hÓgáin). There are also connections with Ciarmait, the 'honey-mouthed' - though it is unclear if these are actually one and the same characters/beings - and the Celtic Ogmios who led his followers with his eloquent words. Ogmios was portrayed, according to the 100s C.E. writer Lucian, as an older man, followed by many, with chains of gold and amber leading from his tongue to their ears.

He gave us the Ogham system of writing, the secret language of the poets, which came into use as we know it around 500 C.E. but is most likely based on a much older system. We have preserved stones with Ogham markings cut into them, mainly names, which may have been territorial boundaries or markers, or memorials to those who had passed. The system is made of a series of strokes that are cut into wood or stone, and the older function would almost certainly have been magical.

One of the recorded uses of the Ogham script is in a story of a message given to Lugh, that was seven strokes on a birch. When read literally this says BBBBBBB. Lugh took the message as a warning; his wife would be abducted seven times into the Fairy realm unless she was protected with birch. This shows there was an element of magic involved in the interpretation of the Ogham scripts, and probably in the making of them. There is another example in one of the texts: The Druid Dallán was sent to search for a person who had been abducted, and despite his best efforts, a year passed with no luck in finding the lady. When he stopped one night on a hill, he turned to the Ogham for aid. 'He made four rods of yew, and marked an Ogham on them, and it was revealed to him through his keys of seer craft and through his Ogham' that the lady in question could be found in an Otherworld dwelling place. Although it doesn't say which symbol the druid used, the Ogham symbol that corresponds to the Yew tree is usually given as Idad, the sound value is I. The particular significance of this combination (yew wood, whichever Ogham symbol he carved, and the number 4, his exact location at the time, plus whatever 'keys of seer craft' or divination he knew to use) may be lost to us now, with much of the Druidical knowledge, but there are contemporary Irish scholars and magicians (such as through the

Irish Pagan School courses, and the excellent work of Irish author John-Paul Patton) crafting a workable revival of the ancient system. It is so much more than a 'Celtic Tree Calendar'!

These examples point to the fact that the Ogham system, even from its earliest inception and recording, was not just used as a convenient means to write your T0-Do list. Some sort of spiritual vision, or magical decoding, was necessary to decipher the true meaning and, following from that, it is logical to assume it could and should be used in the working of magic. That Oghma is credited with the creation of such magical system is indicative of his prominence as a God of magic. Françoise Le Roux, in a speculative interpretation, goes so far as to say he is a God of binding; as the Ogham symbols were in many or even most tales used in such a way as to stay a warrior or an advancing army to a certain task – to bind them to do something. There are quite a few instances of this in the Táin Bó Cuailnge.

One such example is when Cú Chulainn:

> '...arrived at Turloch Caille More ('the Creek of the Great Wood') northwards of Cnogba na Rig ('Knowth of the Kings') which is called Ath Gabla ('the Ford of the Fork'). Thereupon Cú Chulainn went round the host till he came to Ath Grenca. He went into the wood at that place and sprang out of his chariot, and he lopped off a four-pronged fork, root and top, with a single stroke of his sword. He pointed and charred it and put a writing in ogham on its side, and he gave it a long throw from the hinder part of his chariot with the tip of a single hand, in such wise that two-thirds of it sank into the ground and only one-third was above it in the mid part of the stream, so that no chariot could go thereby on this side or that.'
>
> (Táin Bó Cuailgne, Dunn 1914 translation, from 'The March of the Host' section.)

With all the carry on, poetry, and angst that follows with Medb's army trying to get round this seemingly simple obstacle, it seems clear that there's more going on here than the army not having much room to manoeuvre round a post in a stream. So the binding power of the Ogham symbols could be taken as a materialisation of the God's binding powers, I guess?!

Oghma was also known as *Trénfher*, 'strong man', or champion; he was a hero of the Tuatha Dé Danann. He held a valued place in their fighting army and is mentioned often for his warrior prowess. His skills in art were not just those of the scholar and scribe; he possessed much in the way of martial arts talent, as well as his extensive physical power and strength.

The Mórrígan

Modern Functions: Goddess of prophecy and war, inciter of battles. Witch of the Tuatha Dé Danann, weaver of magic to help or harm as she chooses. Keeper of cattle, of the land and water.

Though the Mórrígan is commonly known as a triple Goddess of war, there are actually four Goddess names that are often referred to in this context. These are Mórrígan, the 'Great Queen'; Badhbh (or Badb, pron. Bive), 'Crow or Raven, Scald Crow'; Nemhain (pron. Ne-van), the 'frenzy'; and Macha. All four do not appear together; it is usually only three. The Mórrígan's title is an interesting cover-all to the others, but she also appears as an individual entity. She is the personality most often met in the role of the war Goddess. Dáithí Ó hÓgáin, in his book 'The Sacred Isle: Belief and Religion in Pre-christian Ireland', says:

> *"Manuscripts vary as to the spelling of the first element in her name, and for that reason, it is unclear whether she is originally the Mor-Ríoghain ('phantom queen') or the Mór-Ríoghain ('great queen')".*

It has been suggested that the 'phantom' aspect was a later misrepresentation by christian scribes, who either mistakenly or purposely disregarded the fada (the accent on some vowels in Irish), but also that the word phantom used to mean something a little different than how we consider it now. That the 'phantom' translation may be a misunderstanding, either genuine or specifically to demonise the Goddess, make sense to me personally in light of experiences I have had.

Although I see the Mór-Ríoghain as a sort of cover-all title for the Goddesses of war, one queen to rule them all as it were, as well as a personality in her own right... this is not crystal clear from any of the texts. As mentioned above, there are references to 'the three Mórrígans' in some places. Each Goddess can appear in her own right and often does. Sometimes the Badhbh stands for them all, in their capacity to shape-shift and the propensity for the crow or raven form over a battle. The Badhbh appears in the form of carrion, hooded or scald crow most often, and is also described as 'red-mouthed', perhaps due to the open-mouthed screeching over the battlefield. She is known as *Badhbh Chatha* (pron. Bive Kah-Ha), which means 'the scald crow of battle'.

With regard to her Sovereignty and land connections, the Mórrígan has her own 'paps' (that's boobs, to you and I) in County Meath, by the Brú na Bóinne. As do many, for a few years way back I viewed the Mórrígan as a kill, maim, slaughter kinda Goddess, with not much else to her. As do many, I still felt inexplicably drawn to her even while I was uncertain or even afraid of her in that context. In her Sovereignty role as the Mór-Ríoghain, Great Queen of the land, she can be seen as a protector of the land and its people, who also stands in Sovereignty for the Otherworld. Personally, I feel the war Goddess function is an over-emphasis of one particular aspect of the 'Great Queen' as a whole title and role. It is simply one aspect, or function, that has been singled out.

This ties with the misinterpretation (to my mind) of the word Great as Phantom. A phantom queen, named the Mórrígan, is much easier to demonise and belittle than a respected great queen who holds the political and military protection of the inhabitants of the island of Ireland as a primary function. Of course, this does not mean that the kill, maim, slaughter aspect is not also a significant part of her modus operandi. It very much is. My feeling is that it is simply not the whole of what she is about, as the misconceptions continue today.

The Mórrígan is sometimes seen in her role as the Washer of the Ford, such as when the Cormac - the son of Conchobhar Mac Nessa (Ulster King) - meets the Badhbh washing his bloody chariot in the story of 'The Destruction of Da Coca's Hostel'; signifying that he is destined to die in the forthcoming battle. This role has also survived in a lot of the Welsh literature that deals with the supernatural, probably more prominently than in the Irish. The Mórrígan is also seen in her Sovereign river Goddess association when she meets with the Dagda at the Unius in Connacht.

The war Goddesses themselves rarely (though, not never) physically fight. Their usual function is to inspire terror and dread by their presence at the scene of the fighting. They also use their magic to aid the side they have chosen to give their support to. In the stories, the Mórrígan often appears to be a sort of Witch of the Tuatha Dé Danann, in that she will use her magic to destroy their enemies. She also watches for coming battles and will prophesy the battles and their outcomes. This can be seen in the second battle of Magh Tuireadh. She prepares for seven years and then vows to aid the Tuatha Dé Danann by taking the 'blood of his heart and the kidneys of his ardour' from the Fomhóraigh leader. I could presume that she meant she would take his courage by striking fear into his heart, but you never know with her. It is just as likely she meant to literally rip out his heart and kidneys. And indeed, she does come back with two fistfuls of blood, so...

A notable exception to actually partaking in a fight was when the Mórrígan was crossed by Cú Chulainn in the Táin Bó Cuaịlnge. He refused to sleep with her when she approached him in the form of a comely maiden, 'wrapped in garment of many colours', and offered him union with her. He rejected that by saying, 'I can't attend to a woman at a time like this'. When she offered her help, he replied with: 'it wasn't for a woman's backside that I took on this ordeal!' His loss, right? So, she vowed to hinder him instead. Now, this doesn't mean she was in love with him and was pissed that he had spurned her. Please. If she represented the Sovereignty of Ireland, and it was a leader's duty to pair well with that aspect - sleeping with the Goddess of the land is a common theme in Gaelic Kingship - then his refusal of her aid and herself takes on a whole new meaning. He is showing himself as unfit to rule or lead, but is also holding a position of power. He becomes a threat at that point, and a target.

To hinder him, she appeared in three forms as he fought the Connacht warrior Lóch mac Mofemis. First, as an eel, she wrapped his legs while he was trying to fight. Then as a grey she-wolf, she caused panic in the beasts, so they stampeded against him. Finally, as a red heifer, she led the herds to trample him in the ford. He marked her each time with a wound she could not heal until he gave his blessing on it, but for all her hindrance, he won the fight anyway. Lóch got his head chopped off. The Mórrígan was healed when she tricked him, by giving him three drinks (one from each teat of a cow with three teats, no less). In return, he gave a blessing: 'Good health to the giver!', says he, 'The blessing of God and man on you'. And she was healed, though he soon admitted that if he had known it was her, he wouldn't have done it.

Macha deserves a separate discussion, as she is not just another aspect of the war Goddess. Her main abode and place of connection is the royal court of the Ulster province – Emhain Mhacha, now known as Armagh. Originally the word *emhain* meant 'sacred place or tumulus', and *macha* may simply have meant a 'designated portion of land', which came to be applied to the plain surrounding the Ulster king's holding. Eventually, Emhain Mhacha came to mean the 'tumulus of Macha', and from there a personality became attached to it. There were actually at least three mentions of the name Macha as a distinct mythical personage in the legends. The first was the wife of Nemhedh, a leader of the third invasion of Ireland. He named a plain after her when she died there. The second Macha was a sovereign queen in the same vein as Queen Medb. She married one of her rivals, a man named Cimbaeth, and dominated him, holding the rule of Ireland alone and repelling by her strength those who challenged it. She used her 'feminine wiles' to entice three brothers into bondage and, once she had them overcome, forced them to build the fort at Emhain Mhacha for her royal court.

The third Macha of whom we hear tell was the one who most closely resembles the war Goddess, for she holds great strength and skill in battle, as well as being fleet of foot and full of stamina. In that story, she comes to an Ulster man's household and settles herself in without so much as a by your leave (in other words, without being invited), choosing to stay with him and become pregnant. Crunniuc mac Agnomain was already wealthy, and a widower, but his fortunes increased as she stayed with him. He planned to attend a great fair, and she had warned him not to boast of her to any other. 'It would be as well not to grow boastful or careless in anything you say', said she. He said it wasn't likely. But when he attended the gathering and saw the king's horses racing, he couldn't resist bragging that his wife could outrun them with ease, perhaps forgetting that she was heavily pregnant at the time, but possibly not caring. When the king heard the boasts, the woman was summoned, and none would be satisfied but that she race the horses. 'A mother bore every one of you! Help me!' said she, for she could feel the first pangs of her labour gripping her. Her cries fell on insensitive ears. And so she ran, and she did indeed reach the finish line before the king's steeds. But once there she dropped in pain and gave birth to two babies, a son, and a daughter, and henceforth the place has been named for them, Emhain Mhacha – for *emhain* (pron. ev-enn) in this version means 'twins'. As she screamed out in agony, she laid a curse on the men of Ulster. She said that for nine generations of them, whenever their province was in its direst need, all of its grown men would be as weak as any women in the bed of labour, and this would last for a full five days and four nights. Only three classes of people were exempt from the pangs of Ulster, so it is written: the young boys of Ulster, the women, and Cú Chulainn (possibly due to his Otherworldly aspect). And so it was that when Medb's army attacked Ulster, it was left to Cú Chulainn to defend the province alone, in its time of direst need, against the oncoming Connacht force... a tale well told in the Táin Bó Cuailnge.

The last story of Macha seems to be a surviving remnant of the ancient representation of the land Goddess as a horse, perhaps more prominent in Celtic Europe originally. A horse's abilities would be highly desirable to a tribe, and so came the wedding of the king to the sovereign Goddess of the land in the form of a mare. Medb (pron. May-v) of Connacht was given similar horse significance, and there is a mention of horse racing connected to her role in Tara before she came West. Indeed there is also mention of Liath Macha, the 'grey of Macha': a tremendous chariot horse in the Ulster cycle that, according to one source, was owned by the Goddess herself. Several sources have listed the Mórrígan and Macha as two of a triad sisters, as mentioned previously, and some even seem to suggest that they are one and the same. To my mind, and in my experience, they are quite distinct.

In a modern context, when working with such powers, it is well worth remembering that there is much more to the Mórrígan than the usually represented bitch of blood and battle. However, I don't think I'd be invoking her in a hurry if I needed some tender motherly love. There are others whose main priority that is. If you are finding a maternal relationship with this deity, grand. Understand that that is personal to you, and not how she presents in the lore, or in the land here and now. Please beware of projecting your personal needs or biases onto any deity!

That being said, we should also note what Proinsias MacCana says of the seemingly contrary characteristics to be found within any Goddess legend:

'Maternal, seasonal, warlike, young or aged, beautiful or monstrous... it is significant that in general, each individual Goddess reveals several or all of these characters, and even though one of them may predominate, the others are rarely absent.'

It should be strongly noted that any Goddess, and indeed any God, is a complex web of aspects and connections, often in the unlikeliest circumstances. When working with them, we should take time to get to know them, their history, their affiliations and loyalties, and their intricacies in every way we possibly can. Building relationships is key.

Given here is only a small sampling of the prolific wealth of myth and legend that is available to those interested in the tales of Ireland. The Resources section in this book contains many sources for further research and reading. I have had to leave out vast chunks of our past: the legends of the Táin tales; love stories and stories of disaster and despair; ancient heroes such as Fionn, and his warrior band, the Fíanna. Although you have had but a small taste of what is available, I hope that taste has tickled your palate and left you hungry for more. And when you gain your knowledge, I also hope you share it, for the true pleasure of a tale is in the telling. The myths and legends of Ireland will survive, thrive, and be ever alive, as long as time has an ear and knows an Irish person.

2

Folk and Fairies

Consider the scene, Dear Reader

On a quiet May Day morning, a cottage door silently swings open as the rest of the household sleeps, and a woman slips out and down the path. With a black wool shawl pulled over her head to keep the dawn damp from her hair, she follows the lane until she reaches a gate. Clutching her basket to her chest as she passes through it, she makes her way out across the rough ground, sharp eyes darting from under the shawl to be sure no other watches her make her secret way. She proceeds out of her family's land, crossing the ditch at a dry patch she has found, and finally sets foot on her neighbour's fields. The crops planted in March and April are just starting to shoot a small bit; she notices this with interest as she skirts around the edge of the land - to the same field she was in at the same time, and on the same mission, the previous Bealtaine. Her own family had been losing money every year, as this neighbour's wheat thrived and outdid their own; his bounty was to her detriment. That had stopped last year, and she meant to continue with such a winning formula.

Using the rotten eggs she had brought in her basket, she cursed the neighbour's fortunes at the expense of her own family's, justifying what she did... to herself at least. Mingling the power of her words with the symbolism of her actions, she circled her neighbour's field in a wasteful loop of his former wealth. With that job done, she carefully picked up her basket, removing any obvious traces of her presence from the lightening morning. She slipped back to her own home, smiling in satisfaction at the surety of a more prosperous year to come, now that the competition had been safely taken care of.

You may be forgiven, Dear Reader, for presuming that this tale of magical treachery took place in times long past. I have no doubt that this scene, or versions of it, in fact, did play out regularly way back then. But this particular tale has been gleaned from the occasionally murky vaults of my own family history. The woman in question, *bean an tighe* (pron. Ban on Tee) of a farmhouse in County Clare, was my own Nana's first cousin. She died in 1962 but, to the best of my knowledge, was doing such deeds as long as she was physically able.

Stories such as this are still to be found in many Irish families, in many different forms. Magic has been used by our ancestors with no compunction, no strictures, with only the user's own morals to guide the use. To you and I, this woman could call herself a Witch should she desire. To her, that desire probably would have been very far from her mind. Being named *Cailleach* (hag, witch) in her locality would probably have been an insult of the highest order. Magic and Witchcraft are certainly a fundamental part of the average Irish psyche, but for the most part, they go unrecognised as such.

Or, unspoken, at least.

Family Folklore

When I got the word from the original publishers that I was to go ahead and write this book, there was a great celebration in my family. My Nana was particularly proud of me, as my family had said from the time I was old enough to be scribbling on bits of paper at every available opportunity, and reading anything I could lay my hands on, that I'd make a great writer one day. When I spoke to her on the phone about it, she naturally wanted to know what the book would be about. I told her Irish Witchcraft, and she was down with that - she had attended my Handfasting (Pagan Wedding

Ceremony) in a field a couple of years earlier and blessed herself in the catholic 'sign of the cross' with genuine religious fervour at the sprinkling of the 'holy' water around the circle, bless her cotton socks. Her comment on the book's content was simply, "Well, you should write about what you know". She did want to know though, what would actually be in the book, why it would be 'Irish'. I explained a bit about this part of the book; the history and culture of Ireland as it pertained to the Witch, and of course, Ireland's strong connection with the Fairies. I was genuinely astounded, gobsmacked even, in the truest sense of the word, when she started going on about writing down her stories for me to use as research. "Nana, what stories?" I asked quickly, to stem her midflow from launching into another topic altogether, as she often did. I wanted to be clear I was hearing what I thought I might be hearing. "What stories have you got to write down for me?"

She laughed at me as if I were being silly. "The Fairy stories, of course. And things that used to go around Clare. Wouldn't they help you in your book? I'm sure I can get some more for you too".

It turned out she knew quite a few people from her own generation who were still alive and were only too happy to let me interview them for this book, or others. A whole treasure trove of untapped and unrecorded history and genuine folklore at my fingertips! It wasn't so much that she had the folk and Fairy stories that had so astounded me, it was more the fact that although she knew well I was into Witchcraft, Irish culture, Paganism, and magic - she had known that about me more than 10 years at that stage - she had never thought to tell me about this before. She knew I was majorly interested in magic, and Irish magic particularly, but she simply never thought I'd be interested in her family's and friends' tales. The tales weren't strange to her, whereas, as far as she was concerned, what her eldest grandchild was getting up to has probably fallen into the distinctly strange box from day one, so she must not have put them together. The two just never related in her mind.

And do you know what? I never thought to ask her. I knew she had grown up entrenched in country life, that she has loads of friends who were born and reared in the heart of rural Ireland. Yet I never thought to ask her (or my

Granda, but he was gone at that point) about what they got up to. What tales they told around the fires, what beliefs and traditions they and their parents and their parents' parents carried down - probably stopping only with the mother's or even my own generation. On my part, it was probably pure disassociation with rural Ireland: I grew up in the city, and on our many visits to East Clare over the years we were just that - visitors. Now that I think about it, it's obvious. I should have asked for this sort of stuff years ago. But on Nana's part, the Fairy and folk tales were simply a part of life, as were the traditions and superstitions - an integral part of our psyche, but largely unrecognised as magic or Witchcraft.

A Note for the 2nd Edition:

My Nana passed away in late 2018, and I'm so glad to have this record of some of my time with her. Editing it though, changing things to past tense... that is hard. Rest in Peace Nana.

The Wise Woman

On taking Nana's advice, and talking to people from the county of Clare, one name comes up in nearly every conversation I initiated regarding magic, Fairies, or healing. It is well worth a look at the woman who is perhaps the most easily recognisable name in Irish folklore: Biddy Early.

Bridget Ellen Connors was born in 1798 to John Thomas Connors and Ellen Early, of Lower Faha, about 15 miles from Ennis in County Clare. Although she was married four times, and in those days it was very much the done thing to take your father's or your husband's name no matter what, she was always known as Biddy Early. Her magic was passed through her mother's side of the family, and her name was the link of that. She is, to this day, perhaps the most well-known Fairy or folk healer, wise woman, or Witch in Ireland.

She moved to a cottage in Dromore around 1840, nestled beside a body of water that's called Dromore Lough on the maps, but still known locally as Biddy Early's Lake. Her reputation was already well established at this stage, she was known far and wide as 'The Wise Woman of Clare'. Many clients came to seek her advice, including Daniel O'Connell and an infamous Maureen, the Tinker-Town Queen, and the parents and grandparents of a few I spoke to. Biddy accepted no monetary payment; she only took animals she could use or care of. Brown speckled hens, goslings, roosters, ponies, and pigs were all acceptable forms of payment, as was alcohol and foodstuff.

She was a healer of all ills, great or small. Her famous blue bottle was the source of her healing power, though we can be fairly certain that she carried a fair whack of her own, even without the glass accompaniment. There are many tales, tall tales, and only slightly less tall tales, of how she came by this bottle. Most would agree it was a gift from mysterious strangers who then disappear. There are tales of her being given it by a cradle-bound child, an odd being who could yet play the violin with many strange sounding melodies (that would be a Changeling, in case that's not clear). Her son Paddy may have won it, playing *camánacht*, the ancient and still-popular game of hurling now known as *iománaíocht* (pron. imm-AWN-ee-ockth), for a team of strangers who disappeared afterwards. The tale I heard most often is that of Biddy's cousin, who used the bottle to free a girl from her enchantment and holding in a house (filled with the obligatory mysterious strangers). Where he got the bottle in the first place, nobody seems too sure. The cousin had met these strangers at a crossroads and been taken to dance by them. Learning of the captive girl while at the dance, he determined to free her. The girl's father, a rich Limerick merchant, granted permission for the boy to marry his daughter after he had secured her freedom and brought her home, and he (Biddy's cousin) then passed the blue bottle on to Biddy. Maybe he figured she would find the most use for such a thing, already being a wise woman of some repute. She kept her bottle by her side always, wrapped in a red shawl. She spoke to it and listened closely for the reply, asked of it the future and the present and the past, and got her information every time.

Biddy also had helpers of many sorts. She spoke to Fairies and knew their ways; knew how to handle them, placate them, and frighten them. One girl told me that her granny had gone to Biddy looking for a *piseog* (charm or spell) to free her cat from their torment. Apparently, the poor feline was being driven to dementia by a Fairy who just wouldn't leave it alone. Wetting it seemed to be the favourite trick. The granny had told her that the cat had arrived home soaked to the skin (when there wasn't a drop o' rain to be seen or heard) more times than she could count. She was pretty sure it wasn't local boys, as it happened most often in the night or the evenings when the kids weren't about so much. As most of us will know, a soggy moggy is not a happy cat. Biddy's answer was to tie something (a plant or twig she thought, but she couldn't tell me the name of it) into a piece of string on the cat's neck, worn like a collar. "But not for long, as the cat might get it caught in a ditch on his way through", Biddy said. She also said the cat must have caught hold of a Fairy at some stage, instead of a mouse, and so incurred its wrath. She was to watch it well in the future, and leave the kitchen door open while the house was up and about, so the Fairies could have access in and out if they needed it. Well, it worked anyway. The cat had no more soakings, though it still got more than its fair share of scratches and scrapes that might have been from fighting, or it might have been something else.

Biddy could control the animals by thought alone: "I've 60 sleek sparrows to carry my wishes, my clock is a thistle, my servant a bee" is a quote attributed to her. She was said to have shadows about her house - some form of spirits - who helped her and did her bidding. She called them by their 'family names'.

She was a community carer, in our terms, as she helped and minded many folks who came to her. Mick the Moonlighter was one such case. He had murdered a thieving English landlord, William O'Sheehy, who was sucking the lifeblood from him and his kind. The greedy man had evicted Mick from his house and burned it to the ground, leaving him severely out in the cold, and without hope. So he shot the landlord, as you do. Mick was a cousin of Biddy's, and so turned to her for any help she could give. This was the tail end of the Penal Times in Ireland when we had no rights in our own land, and for such an offense he would surely have been hung without a thought. When he arrived at Biddy's they were already out looking for him with dogs and horsemen. Her advice was to follow the little road to Liscannor, speaking to nobody, and go down along the west coast to Kilrush. He could get a ship from there to America. It is said that she helped him magically. It was the bottle that told her where the men were and when they were coming. She spoke to it then and caused a sleep on the land, and took Mick's sleep from him, so he would have the time and energy he needed to flee. O'Sheehy's men came looking to her door only the next morning, and she was able to tell them that the man they sought was safe on a ship headed out across the sea. Her husband at the time, Tom Flannery, was arrested in his stead, allegedly because they suspected him of being involved or implicated in the landlord's death. The papers at the time made a big deal about the arrest of "Flannery, husband of the 'Witch' Biddy Early". But O'Sheehy's men didn't get to keep their scapegoat. The case was soon dismissed, as Mick the Moonlighter, the man who was solely responsible, was safely in America.

Tom died in 1868 when Biddy was 70, but it was said that she looked no more than 50 years old. I guess consorting with the Fairies can do wonders for a woman's complexion. She married again (yes, at the age of 70) to a man of 30 - in exchange for a cure - but her new husband sickened and died of alcohol poisoning within the year. She wasn't long after him, unfortunately, and died herself in April 1874 (though some sources say '72 or even '73), with her bottle carefully wrapped in its red shawl beside her. The local catholic priest came in, finally laying his hands on the source of her power, and flung it out into the lake. It is said, though, that she had warned the neighbours before she died to throw the bottle into the lake when she was gone, just as the priest had unwittingly done.

And so ended the bodily incarnation of Biddy Early... but her spirit? Her spirit lives on.

The Fairies

Having mentioned the Fairies, let's elaborate on this much talked about but often misunderstood race of beings. The Sidhe (pron. Shee) are the Irish Fairies, fey folk, also known as *Na Daoine Maithe*, or the good people. These beings are not like the flower fairies that have been reported at the bottom of the garden; I don't know what Cicely Mary Barker saw or dealt with, or if she made those flower Fairies up altogether, but they are unlike any sort of Fairy, or even Nature Spirit, that I have ever come across. Maybe I just don't attract the nice friendly sorts, but the traditions of my ancestors (which predominantly focus on protection from and the highest of distant respect for, these Beings) do bear this out. The Fairies I have come into contact with don't hang around under bushes or resting in pretty flowers waiting for you to come and play with them. Some of them do seem to prefer certain plants and trees, but they don't make nests in them. There are no cute little doors into those trees.

They don't have sparkly wings and pretty glittering lace (maybe they do on their own time, but it's certainly not in their job description). I have never, to my knowledge, been hit with 'fairy dust' - to make me sleep, fly, or forget - in all my dealings with the Sidhe. I'm certainly not counting the sparkle dust of those people who go round blowing gold glitter in your face at 'New Age' Pagan gatherings. (That stuff gets everywhere, it's very disconcerting blowing your nose three days after an event and spying sparkling snot on the tissue.)

It is said time and again, by those who would know such things, that the fey or Sidhe are nothing like Tinkerbell, she of Disney's Peter Pan fame. I believe I have even said such myself on occasion, to try and dispel the 'wee cute sparkly Fairy' stereotype. Even if some of them did happen to look like that, I think they would be more like the ones Hoggle is eliminating as pests at the start of the film Labyrinth (from Columbia Tristar Home Video):

Sara, dropping the fairy - 'Ah, it bit me!'
Hoggle - 'Ha huh huh, what did you expect fairies to do?'

But upon further consideration (and much reviewing of said films - all in the name of research, of course), there are actually some similarities. There is a certain petulance, a certain selfishness to the Tinkerbell character, that can be very apparent at times in certain members of Sidhe. There is vanity - the bit in the said film where she stands over the mirror and realises her 'bum looks big in this' is classic - and fat shaming, sending a very wrong message to the young predominantly female audience; which should be noted - and the thoughtless sacrificing of others to get her own desires. In my opinion, the portrayal of the animated character Tinkerbell as such had probably more to do with Disney's unhealthy patriarchal view of women than of any deeper knowledge of the Sidhe; nevertheless, these traits do ring true. Although there are many and varied differences of characteristics within the vast umbrella term that is 'the Sidhe', there are also certain similarities.

The Irish mystic George Russell (known as AE) described them as two major groups - the shining beings and the opalescent beings - as given in W.Y. Evans-Wentz's book "The Fairy-Faith in Celtic Countries". He attributes the opalescent beings a higher status than the shining ones, being the more rarely seen and holding the position of 'great chiefs or princes among the tribes of Dana'. This would tie in with other references to the *Daoine Maithe* (pron. Dee nee Mah-ha) - the Good People - who have also been described as Pagan Gods who lost their status and reverence among humans, or even as fallen angels. They were "next to Heaven at the Fall, but did not fall; they are a people expecting salvation" (Evans-Wentz).

The shining beings referred to would be the regular 'tribe of Danú' or Tuatha Dé Danann. They may have been thought of as beings from other planets. In the Book of Leinster, an Irish Christian manuscript that records much older oral traditions - the Tuatha Dé Danann are described as 'Gods and not Gods'. The Book of the Dun Cow, another Irish manuscript, also has that reference to them. It says as well that they "came from heaven, on account of their intelligence and excellence of their knowledge". The came from heaven bit is a later addition, obviously, than native pre-christian thought and belief, but still goes to show the high regard in which such beings were held.

Fairy Spotting

Working from available source material and commonly held beliefs, it is mighty hard to categorise the Sidhe in any coherent form. There are so many types and descriptions. Most of what appears in this section has been documented before in various places, one source often contradicting another. What I have gathered has been checked, as often as possible, by speaking to people from the areas mentioned and figuring out what they have actually heard of. It relates specifically to Irish folk tradition, though there are similarities with other cultures - most particularly, our close cousins and neighbours, the Scottish.

There are Fairy queens in a lot of areas; perhaps these and their male counterparts are the types of 'opalescent beings' that AE referred to. A queen of the Sidhe was known as *Banríon na Brugh* (pron. Ban Ree-onn nah Broo), 'queenly woman of the palace/hostel'. They are thought to be memories of Goddesses of ancient tribes and are still remembered as guardians of some of the Irish clans.

Áine (pron. Awn-ya) is known from the North to the South. In County Derry, in the North, she is thought to be the progenitor of the O'Corra clann. In County Louth, in the East, she sits at Dunany Point (*Dún Áine*, the strongholds of Áine). Whereas in the province of Munster, in the South, she is well remembered at Knockainey (*Cnoc Áine*, the hill of Áine) in Limerick. She may be a remembrance of the Goddess Anú.

Aoibheal (pron. A-vul) rules from *Carraig Liath* (pron. Car-rig Lee-ah) in County Clare and is the guardian Goddess/queen of the O'Briens of North Munster, who are the descendants of King Brian Ború. She seems to be especially concerned with the future freedom of Ireland, as well as protecting her own people. Her name appears in quite a few of the *Aisling* (pron. Ash-ling) - visionary dreams of the legends.

Cliodhna (pron. Clee-onah) is the ancestral guardian of the O'Keefes and is well respected in Cork. She was the eldest daughter of the chief Druid of the realms of Manannán Mac Lir, who was named Gebann. She is

41

associated with *Carraig Cliodhna* (Cliodhna's Rock), near Mallow in Cork. Lady Gregory tells of her in Gods and Fighting Men (though I must point out, that work is not great source material, for a variety of reasons) in reference to *Tonn Cliodhna*, the wave of Cliodhna. A mortal man, Ciabhan (pron. Kee-van) took her from the Land of Promise, *Tír Tairngire* (pron. Teer Tawrn-geerah), where he was a guest. She had never seen the like of him, for he was a member of *Na Fíanna* (pron. nah Fee-anna) - that is, Fionn MacCumhaill's famous band of warriors. Ciabhan had many skills and talents, as well as his great beauty; he had been booted from Na Fíanna as the other men were upset that all their women gave themselves to him at any opportunity. He must have been really something then, and Cliodhna fell in love, agreeing to leave with him for Ireland. When they arrived, he left her on the shore near Glandore in County Cork while he went off to hunt deer, as was his right. The people of Manannán had followed the pair and sent a great wave to the shore, which carried the Curragh (a type of small boat) with Cliodhna asleep inside it, out to sea, and back to the realms of Manannán Mac Lir.

Úna (pron. OO-nah) was left out of my first book, and that definitely needs to be corrected (and apologised for, publicly - I am SO sorry!) here in the 2nd edition. She has been named 'the last High Queen of the Daoine Sidhe', and you may see her name spelled as Oonagh, Oona, Uonaidh, or Eabhna. She lives at times in Knockmaa with her husband Fionnbheara (see below), but also has her own residence in Tipperary, which is called Knockshigowna today. The name could be from *Cnoc-sidhe-una*, or 'hill of the fairy mound of Una', *Cnocsíghabhna* which may mean 'hill of the fairy cattle pen', or from *Cnocsigamhna*, which would be 'hill of the fairy calf' (thanks to Morgan Daimler for doing the research on the name in their article 'Úna, Fairy Queen of Tipperary' for Moon Books - their book on the Fairy Queens is also an excellent resource!). Regardless, the hill is hugely associated with this Fairy Queen, even to present day it is still as Joyce wrote in 1869 - "the whole neighbourhood teems with fairy names and fairy legends about Una". She has 17 children, according to one story I was told, and I've read they were all sons, bless her. She is a stunner in humanoid form, rocking out shining gold hair that goes all the way down to the ground, and a silver sparkling dress that looks like it's covered in crystal. But she's also a shapeshifter who appears in the forms of a black cat, or a white cow, among others.

And I do believe I now owe her hill a wee visit, so you'll probably be able to find that in my Patreon Site Visit archives at some point!

There were, of course, kings of the Sidhe as well as queens, but these were more in the realm of warrior kings or heroes, than ancestral guardians or Goddesses. Southeast of Magh Tuireadh, where the great battles between the Tuatha Dé Danann and their enemies took place (the first battle was with the Fir Bolg, the second battle was with the Fomhóraigh), and just west of Tuam in County Galway, lies a conspicuous hill - *Cnoc Meadha* or Knockmaa. Atop this hill is an ancient burial place, the dwelling of Fionnbheara (pron. Fee-yun-varra), King of the Connacht Fairies. He loved chess and horses, and rode a black steed with flaring red nostrils - often seen racing through the night alone on his horse, forgoing the usual accompaniment of his host in favour of the thrill of the speedy flight. He also loved to fraternise with mortals, wooing the women away for nights of dancing (unfortunately, NOT always returning them safely to their beds by morning) and inviting the men to ride out with his Fairy host.

Besides these upper echelons of Sidhe society, there are many other sorts and types of Good Neighbours that we come across. The well known Leprechaun (pron. lep-ra-kawn) is very similar to the Clurichaun (pron. Cloor-ih-kawn). In later folklore, both were seen to be dashing wee men in well-tailored suits, and there don't seem to be folk stories about female varieties of either Fairy. But there are references in early texts to the Leprechauns, which are sea dwelling beings (about 18 inches high), and there are some fair wild stories about their Queen and a guy called Fergus. The Leprechaun as we know it, seems to have originated in North Leinster, where they were seen in green-coloured clothing and hats, though there are now many tales of their appearance all over Ireland, and they have become associated with the entire nation in the view of the rest of the world.

A woman in Roscommon related a story to Dr. Hyde (as given in the aforementioned 'Fairy-Faith in Celtic Countries'). She said that in her girlhood, she had been picking wild berries in the ditch when she spotted a Leprechaun in a hole under a stone. She says, "He wasn't much larger than a doll, and he was most perfectly formed, with little mouth and eyes". There was no mention of the fabled purse or pot of gold. However, she does say many told her afterward that she'd have been rich if only she had the sense to catch him. The Clurichaun then are to be found mostly in Munster, wearing hats of red instead of green, guarding (with much sampling of) wine cellars instead of golden treasures. They would seem to be grumpier, drunker, cousin of the Leprechaun.

The *Púca* (pron. Pooka) is perhaps one of the most feared of the Fairies. It goes abroad at night only and can be seen in many different forms. In County Roscommon, it is known as a stamping black Billy goat with great curling horns. In County Laois, it is known as a huge hairy man who will frighten the life out of anybody it meets out after dark. In County Wexford and parts of County Waterford, we hear of a huge dark bird, the shadow of whose wings will cover a whole field. Most often though, it is told that the Púca will be out roaming the night in the shape of a sleek horse, 'black as the divil himself', with wild yellow eyes and a flowing mane. In this form it is said to travel the countryside at night, doing damage to fence and gates, trampling crops, and poisonously spitting on the blackberries once Samhain has passed.

The *Bean Sidhe* (pron. Ban Shee) deserves special mention, even if I don't have the space to go into as much detail about her here as she deserves. Her name means 'Fairy woman', and she seems to be a folk memory of the older battle Goddesses, such as Na Mórrígna, who would foretell the deaths of those about to go into battle, as described in their role as the 'washer at the ford'. There are also hints of ancestral Goddesses, or spirits, as a clann (family) would sometimes have its own *Bean Sidhe*. In Disney's Darby O'Gill and the Little People, she was portrayed as a terrifying hag, combing her hair and wailing at poor old Darby to tell him that his daughter was to be taken. Although Disney may not be best known for its historical accuracy, the portrayal wasn't far off, for she does appear as the hag in some cases. Of course, this is not all she is or can be seen as. As the ancestral entity, she was traditionally only supposed to keen (cry, wail) for five of the primary Irish clans: the O'Briens, the O'Neills, the Kavanaghs, the O'Gradys, and the O'Connors. This select few, I presume, lost their privileges through intermarriage, as in later years many families laid claim to their own *Bean Sidhe*. She is a spirit of the Otherworld, but not sent to kill. Indeed, the folklore idea of her may have come from the major families keeping always a seeress, a woman who was connected with the Otherworld and could walk those paths at will. The wail or keen may have been the warning, or it may have been a method of connection through sound. The *'Bean Sidhe'* of the great houses would provide warning or preparation if one of the family was in danger or inform the rest of the family if something had happened, or was about to happen, to another family member. No mobile phones back then, folks. The Banshee, as she has become known in Irish legend, still comes only to warn the members of her chosen family of their imminent deaths. A useful thing, I would imagine, if not particularly pleasant. If I were about to die, I would certainly prefer to be forewarned and prepared for it, than to leave loose ends and unfinished business - although the tradition is, you don't hear the cry of the Banshee for your own death. I feel it is only in much later years when death and what lies beyond have become things to be afraid of (rather than the necessary conclusion to certain cycles) that the Banshee has developed such a fearsome and frightening reputation of ill omen. The hag appearance is the most oft-reported one, when in fact she could appear also as a comely young maiden or a stately matron.

These are just some of the better-known forms the Fairy folk take in the minds of the Irish. There seems to be a distinction at least between the Tuatha Dé Danann type of regal Sidhe, lords, and ladies of the Otherworld, and the more common local spirits and entities types, who are nonetheless worthy of just the same respect as any others. The commonly known Fairies who inhabit the nooks and crannies of Ireland are not quite the same as Nature Spirits or Elemental energies, though there are similarities. They may be other amalgamations of local lore, shaped from the belief and fear or respect of the community through countless years. They live part in this world and part in the Other. Whether they help us or hinder or us, or even appear to us at all, depends on how they are treated in a long-term fashion, and what they will get in return.

A common theme though, is that everything with them happens on their own terms. So, be warned.

Fairy Fear

In quite a lot of places and families through this land, belief in the Fairies as beings with the genuine power to hurt or heal is still rife. A man I knew spent a lot of time on his family's farm as a child, not far from Tralee in County Kerry. There are many ancient monuments and sites on the land, including a standing stone with Ogham writing on it and a Souterrain (a stone-lined, man-made, underground cave; probably used for storage and protection originally). The passage tomb that lies to the rear of it is the second largest one in Munster. His dad, Bernard, told me that when **he** was growing up, they just called it the Fort. It is about 80 feet in diameter, he reckons, a high hill with a depression around it, and a hollow on the top – probably where some of the passages have collapsed in on themselves over the years. They used to play inside the remaining passages as kids, ignoring the terrible and grave warning they received about playing at the Fort.

> *"They'd tell ye, the Pookies would take ye way", he says, with a self-effacing smile. "That's what they called 'em, the Pookies. An' that they might leave ye back, or they might not. And the Fairy fingers, the flowers, they grew so tall, an' they said they were where the Fairies hid".*

The 'Fairy fingers' are foxglove (*Digitalis Purpurea*) which grow wild in the Irish countryside. They have long been associated with the Fairy folk; some of their other folk names being Foxy Bells, Rosy Fingers, and Fairy Thimbles.

46

That man I knew was a child in the '70s, turning 10 at the end of that decade, and he was told the exact same stories as his dad. I have no doubt, Dear Reader, that if my own children (or grandchildren) were to visit the family farm in County Kerry, they too would be warned of 'the Pookies' by the family there.

Familial Wisdom

In some Irish families, we do see that such things as Fairy lore and folk traditions are not things to be feared; they are highly respected and valued sources of wisdom. Beirn - a powerful woman and dear, respected friend - who is a member of a family of traditional Irish Witches, was good enough to relate to me the following information. I shall leave it in her own eloquent words.

> *"I was brought up with a definite belief in, and sense of the Sidhe – some of my father's people live in Wicklow on a farm near Newtownmountkennedy – until around a hundred years ago it was a pretty much closed community. There were a series of cottages on one side of a mountain and there was the farmhouse, and people didn't actually travel out of their particular valley much. As a result, many superstitions and stories were believed with a fervour unrivalled elsewhere.*
>
> *On the farm was a fairy tree: it was extremely bad luck to touch it, break off any part of it, or disturb it at all. Right up til 1975 my cousins ploughed around it... in 1975 it got struck by lightning and was destroyed! Even then the wood was taken away and burnt ceremoniously. We grew up with endless stories of the Sidhe, their special places, what to do to curry favour with them, what to do to break the curse if you annoyed them, charms, and all kinds of lore about them.*
>
> *When I was a kid I was aware of the Sidhe, not as the kind of Enid Blyton style fairies but as darker, more powerful, more 'noble' entities. I remember being told that the Tuatha Dé Danann were the same as the*

Sidhe, but I don't personally feel quite that. The Old Gods are related to the Sidhe in my opinions, they are all Otherworldly beings, but there are Sidhe, and there are Tuatha Dé Danann – but that's just my view.

I follow the Immramic Meditations and I have meditated in places where the Sidhe are strong. The problem of course with deep meditation outside can be that there are more than a few things one can interact with. There are elementals, genus loci, Sidhe, Land Spirits (what the Norse call Landvaettir) and Gods. But the Sidhe I have found have a particular atmosphere about them, a very definite change in the air when they are present.

I was taught 'ná bhrist tu riomh ná neamhréireacht': to neither bow (literally 'break') before them nor be disrespectful (disagreeing or discordant). I often leave out a token for them, especially if growing spells in the garden or doing something outdoors. In return, I expect a certain amount of interest and goodwill from them when I need it. I respect them, but I don't fear them, I would never make any gesture or act that smacks of worshipping or prostrating myself to them. But I treat them and their places with respect, I know they can harm me, but I can harm them too. They have a lot to teach and are beautiful to know in their own right."

From this, we can see that in some places, such traditions were well respected. And what if they weren't respected? What would have happened then? What revenge would the Fairies take on those who ignored the warnings and disrespected their haunts and ways?

What Fairies Do

The hawthorn, Queen of the May, is a mystical sight indeed (and feared by most folk) when it grows in the Fairy forts. Associated with the letter H, *hÚath* in the Ogham - which has a direct translation of 'horror/terror', and this may not be unrelated?! - Hawthorn is known as an enchanted tree when alone. It is a guardian of the wells and sacred places. I don't think I have ever been to a Fairy fort that didn't have a singular or small group of these wonderful trees. (Okay, they are officially a shrub, and it should be noted, used in hedging quite popularly in the Irish farming communities.) It was known as 'haggard' in the past, and this is the origin of the word hedge. Their prickly branches are a very good barrier to cattle or other farm animals getting out, or intruders getting in.

Live boundaries and hedgerows such as this provide much shelter and variety in the local wildlife, but when the trees grow alone they are said to be the Fairy trees. Farmers would (and still do in many places, as Beirn has described in her family) actually plough around them when they grew in the middle of fields that were formerly grazing land. Anybody who even contemplates taking one down, to build a house or farm through its site, will probably receive a warning or two that bad luck will dog them if they do such a thing. And the funny thing? It usually does, if they ignore the warnings.

The friend of a man I knew, back in the day, received such warnings from quite a few sources, and often from the most unlikely people. You wouldn't know by talking to some people generally that they still held over remnants of their grandparents' beliefs. But they do. This friend ignored all the warnings he received and went ahead and tore down that single hawthorn tree standing alone, so that he could build his house on the site. That particular spot had the best view... apparently, he had bought the land with that view in mind. So, up came the beautiful and ancient tree, ripped from the earth, roots and all, and it was dragged away to be (un-ceremonially) burned. The foundation for the house laid in that spot started to take shape, and then the walls. The build was progressing steadily and solidly until somebody realised that they had somehow gotten the boundaries wrong. The house was being built 2 feet into somebody else's property, and those people were not inclined to sell that particular bit. So, the house had to be knocked down, its foundations ripped from the earth and dragged away. The rebuild started, in the right place, this time with all the boundaries carefully checked. That man was very careful to plant a small but healthy hawthorn tree back in the spot where the original had been ripped up. He lost his view, but his new house was safe.

On any of the Ordnance Survey maps of Ireland we can see any number of old settlements, marked mostly in red and called *Ráth* or Ringfort. These originally were enclosures where people lived, kept their cattle, and kept themselves safe inside earthen mounds, perhaps topped with wooden fences. They can be any size, from enough for one or two huts and some animal enclosures right up to the huge mounds of the royal sites. The smaller ones are often very interesting places to visit, should you stumble across one on a walk in the fields. Although mostly built to house people, for purely mundane or domestic reasons, some were used ritually. Whatever the origins, they have become places of mystery in any locality - once the original settlers were dead and gone.

Here in Ireland, there are beliefs in many areas that the Fairies are departed souls (a belief which I don't personally subscribe to), or at least that those who depart go and live with the Sidhe, ie. in the Otherworld. In Roscommon it is told that many have seen dead friends long after their deaths; both those who have died naturally and those who have been 'taken' by the Fairies (possibly because they died young, before their time?). Though Evans-Wentz lists Douglas Hyde's testimony that in this particular county, folk don't seem to see the Fairies so much as hear or feel them, it seems the Ringforts became associated with the Fairies as they lay empty, with their previous inhabitants having long since shuffled off this mortal coil. The forts are often told to be the dwelling places of the 'good people' and that they often take men and women who happen to stroll by after sunset. I can see why - they are indeed mysterious places when you come across one on a moonlight night, or even more so when the moon is dark. With the reputation of death, snatchings, and perhaps hauntings, with the inhabitants moved on and their spirits forgotten; their former homes were left alone by mortals. Some of the situations of the forts don't seem to make sense from a defensive or an agricultural point of view. Perhaps there were old rivers running that made the areas fertile, or other geographical benefits that have somehow changed since. Or perhaps the ancients built their settlements on or close to natural places of power. When the interlopers died and left, the spirits of the place simply reclaimed what had always been theirs, that which everybody had always known was theirs.

Saying that, why presume the settlers, the builders of these forts, to have been interlopers, unwelcome or unwanted? What of the idea that they were guardians of the places, guardians of the power on the physical plane? When I moved to Roscommon, the theme of guardianship reoccurred time and again when in discussion with various and varied folk who felt drawn to the area, just as I was. The ancient sites seemed to call us.

The Sidhe, it is agreed – both by common cultural wisdom and by the more modern experiences of those who are sensitive to such things – are to be found at the sacred sites of Ireland. There are certain powers that inhabit, that guard, that work with and from certain areas and sites. These are the places that our grandparents avoided walking through, or even near, on the way home from the *Céilí* (pron. Kay-lee) dances. These are the places that a lot of modern Pagan types seek out. Some go home, disappointed and confused that the massive energy surge or spooky experience they were expecting hadn't happened. These are the ones who might tie torn-up pieces of a flowery umbrella to a hawthorn tree outside supernatural caves – just to leave an 'offering' of anything. Bring your rubbish home next time, folks; the Old Ones certainly don't appreciate it. Others wander aimlessly, banging on about 'the natural flow, man', but secretly are unsettled that the odd-looking and untidy pile of dirt they walk back and forth on isn't doing anything for them. They will, of course, go back to where they came from and bang on even more about 'the mystical feel of the homelands'.

Some who visit these places, though, genuinely feel the power that the local spirits keep well hidden from your average Neo Pagan's prying third eye. It's not easily done for the most part. As Beirn recommends, *ná bhrist tú riomh ná neamhréireacht.* A healthy respect for the Fairy spirits, whatever you perceive them to be, is essential. Alcohol, milk, butter, honey, and some of anything you bake are all appropriate offerings to them - but we leave them outside, where we can, rather than invite the Good Neighbours in for them.

51

So many traditions in the households have died out, traditions that kept *Na Daoine Sidhe* satisfied and helpful in return to the householder. But many still survive.

Staying on Good Terms

How many today will apply to the spirits of the place before building a new house or encroaching on their territory? As we have seen, upsetting their natural stomping ground can have disastrous consequences. How is it done?

Traditionally, one had to apply for permission to the Fairies before occupying a newly built dwelling. This was done by placing a bed, a chair, and a small table in the new house, along with plenty of food. This must be done the night before you wish to move into it, and if you arrive back to find the food has not been consumed, with the crumbs swept up by the door, then you don't have their blessing. There have been a few houses to lie empty after such an occurrence, but you may wish to apply to them in other ways instead, bearing in mind the expense of buying or building a house for yourself.

Go to the site. Sit and listen. Close your eyes and feel it. Connect with the land there, and you are halfway to connecting to its guardians. Walk the site. Do you feel led in any particular path or direction?

Look for obvious signs. Trees standing solitary are a dead giveaway, as are patches of particularly wild growth, filled with plants or trees tradition-ally associated with the Fairies: foxglove (Digitalis purpurea), Hawthorn (Crataegus monogyna), blackthorn (Prunus spinosa), elder (Sambucus nigra), brambles (Rubus fructicosus). If anything such as this is present, pay it heed and avoid disturbing if possible. Even if it is nothing else, a patch as described will be a wildlife haven. If the site absolutely must be cleared, replant. Dig up as much as possible and move them to a better location. Plant new versions of what you remove in as sympathetic a way as possible. If doing this, I heartily recommend you make copious offerings of bread, beer, and butter to compensate them for their loss. If they are not happy about you removing their hawthorn, you may end up with (haw)thorns in your bed!

Traditionally; a part of the harvest - whether a yard or two at the end of a drill of potatoes or the last sheaf of corn in the grain field - was left untouched for the *Na Daoine Maithe*. This was sometimes known as the 'Goodman's Croft', left for the Fairies to decide what grew there. You could do the same if you grow and harvest anything around your home, or leave a wild patch as described. Or, pick your patch and populate it with the aforementioned plants and shrubs/trees, then let it grow wild. It is not our land really, after all; we only own it on paper. If there isn't enough land to grow all of the above, at least try and incorporate one or two into your planting scheme or your window box, container garden, or allotment. Anything is possible, and I am sure they appreciate genuine effort and respect as much as any other Being would.

The Fairies are said to despise those who stay up too late at night, or lazy housekeepers – those with 'brockety' shins from spending too much time at their hearth, instead of up and doing in the house and yard. As the housekeeping was usually the responsibility of the women in a household, and few women wore trousers until relatively recently in rural Ireland (many of the older generations still don't); the fire-branded or brockety shins a woman might get from spending too much time sitting in front of the fire - rather than up and doing - were a dead giveaway. The 'Good Neighbours' may give a hand out to a genuinely tired housekeeper, though we are not known for having any sort of house brownies or helpers in Ireland, please note. After the household had gone to bed though, occasionally they may finish the tasks undone that day. This sounds good, but it's never happened to me personally, to date. It is definitely more of a thing in other countries, than in the Irish tradition. But, I wait in hope.

They appreciate a fire that's left stoked up a bit after the household retires, instead of banked down and giving off no lingering heat. So keep a fire stoked up, if you have one, when all are gone to bed, and the Sidhe will find your home a respectful place, should they visit. Leave them the scrapings from the baking bowl, or some other tasty treat, and they will be well pleased, and stay out of your business.

For those who live on foreign soil, the local land or fae spirits may be respected in the same ways. Research any local lore you can find. Talk to older generations who have lived all their lives in an area, and ask if they have ever seen or heard anything unusual about the place. Visit your local library, which often contains pamphlets or booklets locally produced that can be invaluable sources of information on your home ground. In the United States, it is often said that when our ancestors emigrated they brought some of their land spirits or Fairies with them, especially in the larger Irish communities. Check around, and be respectful and aware. Don't presume that just because you aren't on Irish ground that there is nothing Irish to be found.

Of course, in all of this, it is easy to get caught up in romanticism and fancy. For your own sake, and the sake of those who have to listen to you, please keep a healthy dose of reality right at hand. Sometimes a breeze is just a breeze. Sometimes it was squirrels who ate all the cream from the doorstep.

But sometimes, sometimes the Sidhe do show themselves, in subtle ways, and their haunting music can be heard drifting on the evening wind, by those who care to stop and listen.

3

Trials of a Witch's Life

In this chapter, we'll be looking at the Witch in Irish history. We have examined the myths and legends, and we've gained some insight into the fairy tales and folk beliefs - so we have seen *some* of how our ancestors viewed the weavers of magic and those who worked with the Sidhe, in both ancient and more recent times.

None of them would have welcomed the word Witch. But, what about officially recorded history in Ireland? When did the word 'Witch' start being used as an accusation, as an insult, as an incitement to prosecution? What records do we have that show how the authorities, and to a certain extent, everyday folk, viewed the Irish Witch?

Ireland's First Witch?

The most startling thing on the first examination is that there don't seem to have been too many Witches brought to prosecution in Ireland. There is an often-quoted case of Dame Alice Kyteler, notable for the support this lady received from the authorities against her accuser. It is also interesting in that it is one of the first cases in Europe, occurring around the 1300s C.E.

A bishop named Richard de Ledrede, who was an English man by birth, determined in early 1324 that there was a band of heretical sorcerers in

Kilkenny City, led by our own Dame Alice Kyteler. She was a well-to-do lady who had (by then) outlived three husbands, and her fourth was on his way out. She had inherited her late husbands' fortunes and added them to her own family's, and she was considered quite a powerful person at the time. The bishop had held an Inquisition, with pomp and circumstance, and laid out quite a few charges against the good Dame and her crew. These included acquiring the power of sorcery through sexual intercourse with a demon, animal sacrifice, keeping familiars, blasphemous nightly escapades, and of course, inflicting 'death and disease on faithful'. Professor Brian Levack, in his book, 'The Witch-hunt in Early Modern Europe', wrote that:

"the case is a landmark in the formation of learned notions about witchcraft because it reflects for the first time the belief that malefici are organised in a devil-worshipping heretical sect".

After the Inquisition, the bishop wrote to the Seneschal (steward of a medieval great house) of Kilkenny, Arnold le Poer, and the Chancellor of Ireland, Roger Outlawe, who was also Prior of the Preceptory of Kilmainham - both of whom were related to Alice, by the way - asking for the arrest of her crew. They, in return, asked him to drop the charges, or ignore the case.

Thus thwarted, the bishop took matters into his own hands and summoned Dame Alice to appear before him. She ignored him and left the town, headed for Dublin. Thus thwarted (again), he went after her son and alleged second in command, William Outlawe, accusing him of heresy. After William went to his relative, Arnold le Poer, for help (Seneschal of Kilkenny, remember?), the bishop was arrested and lodged in Kilkenny jail himself! This, of course, caused an outcry from the clergy, and the bishop quickly became something of a martyr. And he certainly milked it, but Sir Arnold stuck to his guns and held him until the day when William Outlawe was supposed to appear on charges had come and gone; only then was he released.

The oul bishop was stubborn, you have to give him that much: he immediately cited William to appear before him again. In another weird twist, we then see the bishop himself cited to appear in Dublin to answer for

56

having placed an interdict (a prohibition on church activities, which he had placed as soon as he had been locked up in jail) on his diocese. He got out of that one by pleading danger to his life, as he would have passed through hostile lands to get to Dublin to stand trial.

There were various to-ing and fro-ing after this. At one time Sir Arnold publicly alluded to the bishop as a 'vile, rustic, interloping monk', and eventually Dame Alice became involved again. She had been making friends in Dublin and had the bishop summoned there to answer charges, the bottom line of them being that he had falsely accused her of sorcery. He went, he talked a lot, and it ended (so it seemed) with himself and Sir Arnold mutually giving each other a 'kiss of peace'. When he returned his attention to the good Dame once again, she neatly escaped all further trouble by departing for England, and presumably spent the rest of her days there in peace; at least, we never hear of her again. It was her poor crew that bore the brunt of the bishop's wrath from then on, and, with them not having the same clout as she, they really suffered.

Ten names are recorded: Robert of Bristol, a clerk; John Galrussyn, Ellen Galrussyn; Syssok Galrussyn; William Payn de Boly; Petronilla of Meath; her daughter Sarah; Alice, the wife of Henry Faber; Annota Lange; and Eva de Brownestown. They all confessed to his charges and more, after a personal visit in prison from him (we know that repeated flogging/whipping – at the very least – was used as a form of torture in the case of Petronilla), but the proper authorities weren't interested in detaining them permanently, owing mainly it seems to William Otlawe's continuing influence and protection.

Eventually, the bishop went to the Justiciary and obtained his 'justice'. They were all formally detained, and the Justiciary promised to deal accordingly with them on his next visit to the town. On this, the bishop formally accused William of no less than 34 charges – among them clericide, adultery, and usury (which is the act of lending money with interest, usually exorbitant interest), as well as the more common or garden variety 'heresy and the defence of heretics' charges.

When all this was finally brought before the Justiciary, Dame Alice was found guilty, despite her absence, of sorcery and heresy. William was eventually brought on bended knee before the bishop, who made him promise to re-roof in lead one church and part of another, attend at least three masses a day for a year, and feed a certain number of poor people. He didn't meet these penances, and ended up in prison. Of the rest of the band, we know for sure only the fate of Petronilla of Meath, who was the maid to Dame Alice Kyteler. This unfortunate young woman was flogged continually until she confessed to various magical acts, and she became pretty much the scapegoat for her mistress. Petronilla was burned alive in Kilkenny town on Sunday, November 3, 1324. It was the first time such a punishment had officially been used in Ireland for heresy or sorcery.

Ultimately, the bishop got his comeuppance, as he himself was subsequently accused of heresy, twice. He denied it all, and avoided any formal punishment, but had all his goods seized twice over the years, and endured much hardship and poverty until 1360 when he finally died. Is it just me, or does that seem like an awful amount of bad luck for a powerful man to have suffered? An unnatural run of luck, perhaps?

There were many factors that led to Dame Alice Kyteler's accusation. She was disliked by the disinherited and disgruntled children of her former husbands. There was some sort of general malice toward her and William, as they were heavily involved with money lending, which created quite a lot of tension. Another point of interest is that the bishop of Ossory came into his power just as a new catholic pope – John XXII – came to his. This man was quite paranoid about Witchcraft, believing himself to be constantly under attack from enemies who modelled wax images of him, sent him enchanted jewellery, and various other sorceries. So once he became pope he began giving official stamp and license to Inquisitors and recognising the power and danger of magic users in his various papal bulls of the time. The bishop was a firm believer that the church was a law unto itself, and unquestionable by state officials, and so he may have been trying to curry favour in Rome or make a name for himself – or trying to prove that what the church/pope said was happening, was actually what was going on.

So was the sorceress of Kilkenny actually a Witch, as we understand it? There is an instance recorded of her having "swept the streets of Kilkenny between compleine and twilight, raking all the filth towards the doors of hir sonne William Outlawe, murmuring secretly with hir selfe these words…

'To the house of William my sonne
Hie all the wealth of Kilkennie towne'."

Even taking the other factors into account, this may be an indication that Dame Alice was indeed a user of magic. Of course, it may not. I will leave it up to you to decide, Dear Reader.

Who Else?

Although Petronilla was the first, she was not the last to be burnt for heresy or sorcery. Most of the charges (the ones we know of, at least) against the following unfortunates seem to consist of not following along with the teachings of the catholic church: denying the doctrines of the Trinity, not believing that Jesus was the son of God and declaring him a mortal and a sinner, worshipping the Virgin Mary (as a Goddess figure?), following various Pagan superstitions and drawing the 'faithful' off with them.

Among those sentenced to be burnt for these 'crimes' were the eloquent poet Adam Dubh O'Toole (of the Leinster O'Tooles, in 1327). This man met his end for the crime of heresy at College Green in Dublin in a public lesson to others by the christian church. His official charge was along the lines of 'denying the doctrines of the Incarnation of the Holy Trinity, and rejecting the authority of the Holy'.

There were also some accused who came from the diocese of Ossory (yes, him again), who I can only presume were part of the Dame Alice saga or a legacy of the same bishop, as there is no more information on them that I could find. In Robbins Encyclopedia, he gives the date as 1327: burnings for heresy, in Kilkenny. That may have been the remnants of the Dame Alice crew.

There were two men from Bunratty tried in Country Clare, then put to the flame, in 1353. There were a few more in Kilkenny, quite a bit later in 1578. Two Witches and a 'blackmoor' are recorded to have been burned, and some 36 others hailed for heresy. There is a rumour that these 36 others were put to death, but I have found no evidence to support this. And that's pretty much it for the recorded cases of death by fire for the charge of heresy in Ireland. Not a lot, considering the wave of hysteria that was spreading through Europe at the time.

Aside from trials of the period 1300-1330, which were mainly concerned with political sorcerers and had other socio-political implications and involvement, there are very few actual Witch trials in other countries that were any earlier than that of Dame Alice Kyteler, which was in itself more reminiscent of the sorcery trials than the Witch hunt of later periods, and none so well documented.

There is the report of an English case of a woman in 970 CE, who was accused of attempting to murder her victim by driving pins into a puppet made in its likeness. The accused was drowned at London Bridge after her trial. However, as we have examined, Dame Alice was not accused or persecuted by an Irish man, but by a foreigner. Indeed, many or most of the trials were brought about by non-Irish accusers. So although her case is one of the earliest recorded, it certainly does not reflect the overall mentality of the Irish people.

The worst period of activity regarding trials for actual *maleficia* (malicious acts attributed to Witches) in the rest of Europe seems to have been around 1580 - 1650, with the time of 1610 - 1630 CE being the most active in terms of Witch hunting, in the opinion of Professor Brian Levack. Right in that time-frame fell the Bamberg trials, in Germany, which started in 1609 and went right on until 1631, when ever-increasing political pressure forced changes to the madness of the situation. Professor Levack gives a very tentative estimate of perhaps 110,000 prosecuted, with maybe 60,000 of those ending in executions, during the 16th and 17th centuries. Now, compare this to Ireland.

How many Witches were tried in the period of 1580-1650? One: John Aston, in 1606. And during the 1400s and 1500s generally, when so many across Europe were being killed on such charges, how many in Ireland? At the highest estimate I have seen, it was 39, but that is including those aforementioned 36 people in 1578 in Kilkenny, a case in which nobody seems too sure what the outcome was. If we were to count these, well, it is still only 39. To be completely fair and impartial, let's say we take into account that Ireland is an island, and that (even now) everything seems to arrive here later than anywhere else – lying as we do at the last bastion before the Great Pond of the Atlantic. Let's give the grace of the following period, that of the 1600s. We see how many more, in the race to catch up with the rest of the world?

The trial of Florence Newton, the Witch of Youghal, occurred in 1661 in the midst of a colony of Puritans who had settled there in Cork. She was an old woman, and the trial had all the hallmarks of European madness stamped on it – with the victim's vomiting of needles, pins, horseshoe nails, wood, and straw, with the small stones following the victim from room to room and hitting her head and arms, with the lifting of the victim out of bed and right up to the roof of the house. How many fell prey to this madness, how far did it spread in the community? Anybody who has read accounts of the Continental or Salem trials will know just how quickly and frighteningly such things can get right out of hand. In Youghal, though there were plenty of witnesses, Mistress Newton was the only one who stood trial. She herself accused two others as co-conspirators (Mistress Halfpenny and Mistress Dodd), but these two ladies were cleared of any wrong-doing by the victim herself. It is uncertain as to the outcome of the trial or the final fate of Florence Newton. If she was executed, we can add one more to the number of Irish Witches put to death in this period. Have we any more?

There is a report of a woman who had supposedly used a sorrel leaf to bring on convulsions and fainting in a young girl (plus the usual mind-bending vomit of various household and farmyard objects) in Antrim in 1698. It says the Witch was apprehended and refused to recant, so she ended up strangled and then burned. This just scrapes into the 1600s bracket. Still, not exactly hitting near the 60,000 mark here, are we?

The last trial of this ilk was as late as 1711, again in Country Antrim, near Carrickfergus. This is the Island Magee case, a report of which was printed in a pamphlet circulated from Belfast in 1822. It centres around a Presbyterian minister's wife and her household, and tells of many strange goings-on involving apparitions of a young boy, talk of the devil, stolen books, bedclothes being messed with repeatedly, and lots of allusion to death and corpses. When the wife eventually died, it was said that she was bewitched to death, and this seemed to have a startling effect on a subsequent guest to the house, 18 year old Mary Dunbar. This girl started to have fits nearly immediately on her arrival and was able to describe a vision of a group of seven or eight women talking together and calling each other by name.

Thus the names of seven local woman were brought into the affair: Janet Mean, Jane Latimer, Margaret Mitchell, Catherine M'Calmont, Janet Liston, Elizabeth Sellar, and Janet Carson. There are many charms and spells ascribed to the Witches and described in the trial account, most involving knots in yarn, clothing, and materials. "Seven double knots and a single one" seems to have been the favourite. There is even a counter-charm, used on the advice of the local catholic priest, involving words from the Gospel of St. John and a tape with its own knots, which was tied around the girl's neck. This seems to have been turned against the victim, as it was subsequently found to be tied around her middle, causing her immense pain, with no rational explanation of how it got there – according to several witnesses. Miss Dunbar was also said to have done the vomiting trick, with feathers, cotton, yarn, pins, and two large waistcoat buttons produced as evidence.

All of the accused women denied the charges and had no lawyers to defend them, and there was no medical evidence given in court. Their characters were brought into question during the trial and were declared unfavourable in some cases, seemingly due to their supposed ill appearance rather than any actual misdeeds. Nearly all of them were regular church attendees. One of the case judges, Judge Upton, was of the opinion that if the accused were indeed Witches, "in compact with the Devil", they would hardly have been so constant in their churchgoing. He was also of the opinion that the women could not be found guilty on the evidence of the young girl's visionary images. The other judge, Judge Macartney, was not quite so open-minded. He recommended that the women be brought to immediate justice, which the 12 men of the jury promptly did. In the face of such hard-hearted judgement, you might be forgiven for worrying as to the fate of the seven women. They might well have followed the fate of some of their predecessors and been strangled and burned. Not exactly.

Perhaps it was due to Judge Upton's more lenient attitude, but their fate was a mere one year imprisonment. Not an easy time, I would imagine – especially when we take into consideration that four times during their year's sentence they were forced to stand in pillory (a wooden framework with holes for the head and hands, a sort of stockade) in public and be pelted by their neighbours with eggs and cabbage stalks. One of the women lost an eye on one occasion when the mob got quite caught up in the process. I am sure those women suffered many hardships during their year in prison. On the whole, however, I would imagine, it was a whole lot better than being crispy fried on a bonfire.

And so ends the final official Irish Witch trial. No horrendously high figures to tally up, no claims of mass murder by mob rule, no real hysteria outside of the odd little crank here and there who couldn't keep their pins and feathers in their stomach where they belong. We see the occasional interesting record of charms, incantations, and grouping of people, who may or may not have been working together and using such charms and incantations, sometimes for their own gain, sometimes to the detriment of their neighbours, and sometimes for payment.

In Ireland, we generally escaped the notice of the keen Witch hunters across the waters, including that most vociferous of monarchs King James VI... and didn't seem to breed any Witch hunters of our own. Our Parliament passed only one statute on Witchcraft, ever, and as far as I know, it has never been repealed or even addressed, so is probably still theoretically in force.

In modern terms, much of it would go against a person's constitutional right for religious and personal freedom, so I can't see a classical Witch trial going on today or tomorrow. And since the formation of ATC Eire, on February 24, 1999, Wicca at least is a legally recognised presence in this country. On October 1, 2001, the Rev. Barbara Lauderdale, who was president of ATC Eire, received notice of official registration as the first Wiccan church to be recognised by the Irish government. This would be something to refer to, at the very least, in a modern discriminatory case against a Witch.

A Note for the 2nd Edition:

Since this book was first written, Pagan Life Rites (Ireland) have received official and legal recognition by the Irish Government, co-founded by myself and a team of amazing, dedicated colleagues. We have appointed a number of Reverend legal celebrants within the ranks of our Clergy, who can perform state recognised marriage ceremonies, as well as being available for a number of other social or community causes and functions.

The Law

Even as Witch laws go, the old law here was fairly mild; with no allowance being made for torture and the punishment being the relatively more humane hanging, drawing, and quartering for males, and burning after strangulation for females. The same as was doled out on convicted felons at the time, in fact. It should be noted that the penalty of death was not passed for being a Witch or being involved in Witchcraft, only for causing death by Witchcraft. The law runs as follows, as given by St. John Seymour in 'Witchcraft and Demonology':

> *... a Statute was passed by the Irish Parliament in 1586. Shorn of much legal verbiage the principal points of it may be gathered from the following extracts:*
>
> *'Where at this present there is no ordinarie ne condigne punishment providen against the practices of the wickes offences of conjurations, and of invocations of evil spirites, and of sorceries, enchauntments, charms,*

and witchcrafts, whereby maine fantasticall and devilish persons have devised and practised invocations and conjurations of evill and wicked spirites, and have used and practised witchcrafts, enchauntments, charms, and sorceries, to the destruction of the persons and good of their neighbours, and other subjects of this realm, and for other lewde and evil intents and purposes, contrary to the laws of Almighty God, to the peril of their owne soules, and to the great infamie and disquiteness of this realm. For reformation thereof, be it enacted by the Queen's Majestie, with the assent of the lords spirituall and temporall and the commons in this present Parliament assembled.

'1. That if any person or persons after the end of three months next, and immediately after the end of the last session of this present parliament, shall use, practise, or exercise any witchcraft, enchauntment, charme, or sorcery, whereby any person shall happen to be killed or destroied, that then as well any such offender or offenders in invocations and conjurations, as is aforesaid, their aydors or councelors... being of the said offences lawfully convicted and attained, shall suffer paines of death as a felon or felons, and shall lose the privilege and benefit of clergie and sanctuarie; saving to the widow of such person her title of dower, and also the heiress and successors of such a person all rights, titles, & c., as though no such attaynder had been made.

'2. If any persons (after the above period) shall use, practise, or exercise any witchcraft, enchauntment, charme, or sorcery, whereby any person or persons shall happen to be wasted, consumed, or lamed, in his or their bodie or member, or whereby any goods or cattels of any such person shall be destroyed, wasted, or impaired, then every such offender shall for the first offence suffer imprisonments by the space of one yeare without bayle or maineprise, and once in every quarter of the said yeare, shall in some market towne, upon the market day, or at such time as any faire shall be kept there, stand openlie in the pillorie for the space of sixe houres, and shall there openly confesse his or theire errour and offence, and for the second offence shall suffer death as a felon, saving & c. (as in clause 1.)

'3. Provided always, that if the offender in any of the cases aforesaid, for which the paines of death shall ensue, shall happen to be a peer of this realm: then his trial therein to be had by his peers, as is used in cases of felony and treason, and not otherwise.

'4. And further, to the intent that all manner of practice, use, or exercise of witchcraft, enchauntment, charme, or sorcery, should be from henceforth utterly avoide, abolished, and taken away; be it enacted by the authority of this present Parliament that if any person or persons... shall take upon them by witchcraft, & c., to tell or declare in what place any treasure of gold or silver shall or might be found or had in the earth or other secret Places, or where goods or things lost or stolen should be found or become, or shall use or practice any sorcery, & c., to the intent to provoke any person to unlawful love (for the first offence to be punished as in clause 2), but if convicted a second time shall forfeit unto the Queen's Majesty all his goods and chattels, and suffer imprisonment during life'.

There was one other act of Parliament that mentions Witchcraft, in which it lists bewitchment as a way to kill a person. Again, quoted from 'Witchcraft and Demonology':

Forasmuch as the most necessary office and duty of law is to preserve and save the life of man, and condignly to punish such persons that unlawfully or wilfully murder, slay, or destroy men...and where it often happeneth that a man is feloniously strucken in one country, and dieth in another county, in which case it hath not been found by the laws of this realm that any sufficient indictmeny thereof can be taken in any of the said two countries...For redress and punishment of such offences... be it enacted...that where any person shall be traitorously or feloniously stricken, poysoned, or bewitched in one country (and die in another, or out of the kingdom, &c.), that an indictment thereof found by jurors in the country where the death shall happen, shall be as good and effectual in the law as if, &c. &c.).'

Although there were very few recorded events in this time period, it may be supposed that some went on that were never recorded, or that records made at the time have been subsequently lost. Maybe others were burnt, hanged, or strangled to their death for Witchcraft or heresy in villages and towns all through the Irish land. The English in Elizabethan times who lived here in Ireland, when their cattle were afflicted with a disease that sent them blind, blamed Irish Witches, calling them eye-biters. Apparently they "did commonly execute people for it".

Much of what occurred - the main trials, the executions, and the laws - doesn't seem to have been at the instigation of the native Irish. It should be pointed out that this may be due to the refusal of the Irish to bring charges in courts operating under English law. As far as we were concerned, the Brehon (native Gaelic) laws were abided and judged by, not the laws imposed by the English. There have been many invasions of our soil and turmoil through the years, as most of us are aware, and much of what occurred regarding Witch trials seems to have been brought in, as I have already said, by Puritan settlers and others of the same sort. The native Irish, I feel, certainly practiced magic of all kinds; they were both nice and nasty to each other, and to those who came to live among them. They carried on with the things they had been doing for many years, their own 'superstitions', their own beliefs and ways. Belief in the reality and powers of *Na Daoine Sidhe*, ghostly beings and spirits, the closeness of *An Saol Eile*, the 'devil' (seemingly as a malevolent natural being), and of course magic, both hurting and healing, were widespread. So, even given the lack or loss of records, refusal to initialise prosecutions and rebellion against outside influence, a case may be made that in Ireland, the use of magic was inherently more acceptable than it was elsewhere.

Ireland's Failed Witch

An interesting trial regarding Witchcraft and the use of magic in Ireland, even if it wasn't an actual 'Witch trial' (no vomiting of pins or feathers or anything), was held in the Spring Assizes in Carrickfergus, County Antrim, in March 1808.

This was the trial of a woman named Mary Butters, of Carmoney, who was a local wise woman by reputation. I find this particular trial fascinating when compared to others that were occurring around the same time period elsewhere in Europe, such as the slightly earlier (it takes a while to get here, remember) 1782 trial of Anna Göldi in Glarus, Switzerland. The most fascinating thing about the comparison is the reaction of the people in the Irish community to what was blatantly and obviously the working of charms and spells, the use of magic, and, therefore, Witchcraft.

The church had a firm grip on Ireland, officially that is, by the time the events that led to this woman's trial were recorded publicly in the Belfast Newsletter (Carrickfergus is just north of Belfast, in what is now known as Northern Ireland) of August 21, 1807, and also in 'Historical Notices of Old Belfast' by M'Skimin. Was there a public outcry? A lynch mob? Was the man who had hired the Witch in the first place charged with any sort of misdeed? Did local folk, or even the local priest, report the occurrences to Rome for an official investigation?

Well, no actually. A local wag wrote a scathing (and rather funny) satirical poem about all involved. Mary Butters and the man who had hired her were pretty much the laughingstock of Carrickfergus.

The Ballad of Mary Butters (Author Unknown - deliberately!)

In Carrick town a wife did dwell
Who does pretend to conjure witches,
Auld Barbara Goats, or Lucy Bell,
Ye'll no lang come through her clutches.
A woeful trick this wife did play
On simple Sawney, our poor tailor.
She mittimissed the other day
To lie in Limbo with the jailor.

This simple Sawney had a cow,
  Was aye as sleekit as an other;
  It happened for a month or two
  Aye when they churned they got no butter.
  Rown-tree tied in the cow's tail,
  and vervain glean'd about the ditches;
  These breets and charms did not prevail,
  They could not banish the auld witches.

The neighbour wives a' gathered in
  In number near about a dozen;
  Elspie Dough and Mary Linn,
  An' Kate M'Cart, that tailor's cousin.
  Aye they churned and aye they sweat,
  Their aprons loos'd, and loost their mutches;
  But yet nae butter could they get,
  They blessed the cow but curst the witches.

Had Sawney summoned all his wits
  And sent away for Huie Mertin,
  He could have gall'd the witches' guts,
  An cured the kye for Nannie Barton.
  But he may show the farmer's wab,
  An' long wade through the money gutters;
  Alas! It was a sore mis-job
  When he employ'd auld Mary Butters.

The sorceress opens the scene
  With magic words of her invention,
  To make the foolish people keen
  Who did not know her base intention
  She drew a circle round the churn,
  And washed the staff in south run water,

And swore the witches she would burn,
But she would have the tailor's butter.

When sable night her curtain spread
   Then she got a flaming fire;
   The tailor stood at the cow's head
   With his turn'd waistcoat in the byre.
   The chimney covered with a scraw
   An' every crevice where it smoak'd,
   But long before the cock did craw
   The people in the house were choak'd.

The muckle pot hung on all night,
   As Mary Butters had been brewing
   in hopes to fetch some witch or wight,
   Whas entrails by her art were stewing.
   In this her magic a' did fail,
   Nae witch nor wizard was detected,
   Now Mary Butters lies in jail
   For the base part she has acted.

The tailor lost his son and wife,
   For Mary Butters did them smother;
   But as he hates a single life
   In fur weeks time he got another.
   He is a crouse, aul canty shiel,
   An' care nae what the witches mutter;
   He'll never mair employ the Deil,
   Nor his auld agent Mary Butters.

At day the tailor left his post
   Though he had seen no apparition,
   Nae wizard grim, nae witch nor ghost,

Though still he had a stray suspicion
That some ould wizard wrinkled wife
Had cast her cantrips o'er poor Brawney
Cause she and he did live in strife,
And wha's the man can blame poor Sawney.

Wae sucks for our young lasses now,
　For who can read their mystic matters,
　Or tell if their sweethearts be true,
　The folks a' run to Mary Butters
　To tell what thief a horse did steal,
　In this she was a mere pretender
　An's has nae art to raise the Deil
　Like that ould wife the Witch of Endor.

If Mary Butters be a witch
　Why but the people all should know it,
　An' if she can the Muses touch
　I'm sure she'll soon descry the poet.
　Her ain familiar off she'll sen'
　Or paughlet wi a true commission
　To pour her vengeance on the man
　That tantalises her condition.

This poem is proof that the memory, at least, of the power of the *File*'s satire was alive and well in Ireland at the time. To explain the story a bit better for those of us not outstandingly proficient in ye olde poetry....

The man who had hired Mary Butters was named Alexander Montgomery, known locally as Sawney. He was a tailor, married with one son. Besides his tailoring, he also kept a few cows. One of his cows was giving plenty of milk, but for some reason, they couldn't make any butter from the milk she gave. His wife reckoned the cow was bewitched, and they tried a few simple charms to try and break her free from the enchantment. They tied a few sprigs of the rowan tree, or mountain ash, with its red berries, into the cow's tail. They tried vervain, which is a native wild plant, too. These are traditionally potent anti-Witchcraft charms thought to be very protective, but (perhaps because they only turned to magic after the fact) the protective powers weren't coming into force. None of it was working for them.

It is also interesting that the tailor's wife had only been speaking to local wives and women at this stage, and they knew enough of basic protective energies between them to recommend these initial simple steps. They gathered in the tailor's house and talked and worked. But, even though they blessed the cow and cursed the witches, the milk would still yield no butter, regardless of how long they churned. The tailor's wife then learned that a wise woman, the aforementioned Mary Butters, may be able to help.

The wife sent her husband off to fetch the wise woman, and she arrived at their house (this was a night in August 1807). She started work about 10 o'clock that night, with much muttering of 'magic words', to impress the people gathered. Present that night were another old lady by the name of Margaret Lee, thought to be a helper or friend of Mary Butters'; a young man named Carnaghan (likely a farm hand or such); Alexander 'Sawney' Montgomery; his wife and their son. Mary was said to have drawn a circle around the offending butter churn and washed its staff (the stick with which to beat the butter) 'in south ran water'. She then swore to beat the Witches at their own game and to have the tailor's butter before dawn.

The men were sent out to the cow-house and given strict instructions. They had to turn their waistcoats inside out and stand by the head of the cow until Mary sent for them, and they were not to stir before that. The women and child stayed in the house, where the chimneys were blocked up - along with every gap, window, and crack she could find. Into the cooking pot over the roaring fire, she put some of the cow's milk, some needles, pins, and some crooked nails. She probably had the like of the rowan berries and various other protective herbs added to the cauldron pot too. Sulphur of some description managed to make its way into the mixture, along with all the rest of the ingredients. Magical ingredients they may have been, but no magic will work without a healthy dose of common sense. And no magic will protect you from sulphurous fumes.

The men outside got progressively more worried as the night wore on, and by the time dawn arrived they mutually agreed to abandon their post, so as to see what was happening inside. The doors were locked in the house, and through a small darkened window they could see the occupants stretched out on the floor inside as if they were dead. Horrified, they broke down the door, and when they rushed into the room they found that the tailor's wife and his son were, in fact, dead, with the two other women nearly following in their wake. Indeed, as they checked on everybody, Margaret Lee died there and then, but they kicked Mary Butters until she came to.

The story she told them then was fantastic, concerning a dark man with a huge club who had come in, killed all three and stunned herself - sent by or on behalf of, no doubt, the evil Witches she was hoping to banish.

She was brought to trial, as I have mentioned, at the Assizes that Spring, having spent the interim languishing in jail. And what was the final fate of Mary Butters, failed Witch and laughing stock of the town? She was 'discharged by proclamation'.

The Magic Still Lingers

They were very few cases after all this, that even mentioned Witchcraft or magic. Biddy Early, who we met in Chapter 2, had many run-ins with local priests. They were appalled by the level of respect and attention given to her by their parishioners. In 1865 she was brought to Ennis and charged with Witchcraft under the 1586 statute mentioned previously. The case was dismissed by a local judge "due to lack of sufficient evidence against the accused". There were a few who had been talked into giving evidence against her by the clergy; their evidence never materialised. I guess they knew in their hearts where the loyalty lies, or else they were just scared of her!

A woman named Bridget Cleary, in 1894, disappeared from her home in

Ballyvadlea, near Cloneen in County Tipperary. Rumours of foul play flew, and it all came out in the wash when her body was found a few days later. It had been buried all drawn up in a cramped position, in a bog not far from her house.

On examination, it was pronounced that her death was caused by extensive burns she had received. Her husband, her father, her cousins, and some of her friends - eight people in all - were brought before magistrates to stand charge for her murder. The primary perpetrators were her husband, Michael Cleary, and her father, Patrick Boland. They had burned her in her own hearth fire. After months of ever-increasing madness and torture sessions, in which the two men became increasingly convinced that it wasn't their wife/daughter they had at all, but a Witch or (more likely, to their minds) a Fairy Changeling, the final act of throwing her on the flames was to drive the Fairies from the house and return their Bridget to them. A horrendous and chilling example of myth (and man) gone mad, but not a Witch trial in itself.

Writers on the subject of Witchcraft history will often examine English and Scottish cases and thoroughly glide over Ireland. This is due in part to the geographical isolation of the island. (There were no ferries back then, Dublin to Holyhead in 20 minutes was not even a twinkle in the eye of the enterprising.) It is also due, no doubt, to the fact that there is so little actual evidence and material available on the Irish Witch trials (relatively speaking). Perhaps there were more records, which have been lost. Perhaps the lack of evidence is due simply to the lack of circulated written material to add any fuel to the fire of ordinary folks' imaginations. Trials that did occur were not generally recorded on pamphlets and circulated sheets for public consumption as happened in the rest of Europe.

The dearth of Witch trials in Ireland is also - and, Dear Reader, of this I have no doubt - due to the fact that the native Irish have such an ingrained acceptance of magic in all its forms, that we simply didn't look for Witches at every drop of a butter churning staff. The prevailing attitude was far more likely to have been along the lines of - "sure maybe the good folk are not best pleased with us right now, we'll leave some o' the butter out for 'em tonight an see how we go".

If the average Irish person in the 1500s or 1600s suspected a neighbour of using malevolent magic against them, they would pay a little visit to the local friend of the Fairies, the wise woman or man, and ask for a bit of help to sort things out. They fought like with like. Hard as it may be to believe in today's dear old catholic Ireland, the church back then didn't seem to have had the same sort of rigid grip on the land or the people in the reality of day-to-day life. The Papal Bulls denouncing Witchcraft and heresy may have affected and inspired high-ranking folk such as the bishop of Ossory, but the average person living and working in Ireland didn't have a clue (or really even seem to care) what a pope in Rome might think or say. The magic is here, we all know it is here, and those who want to use it are welcome to it. It's not something we think about or worry about or even talk about for the most part. It just is.

"[B]ut it was not until I returned to Ireland that I discovered that the borders between our world and the Otherworld are not as substantial as they seem. There is something about this land, something we do not feel because we are so close and bound so strongly to it. The strangers and visitors here feel it, in the air and on the wind; it is as if the magic still lingers". - Michael Scott, Irish Folk and Fairy Tales.

II

How It Is

4

Land and Gods

This chapter is one of the most personal to me. This is Ireland at its core. This is where the magic lies in all its glory: the land and its Gods, Guides, and Guardians.

The first step in the connection process is your immediate surroundings: your home, your area, your community, your county. This applies, wherever you are in the world - you need to learn to connect to the ground on which you stand. Look at what's around you. In Ireland, we don't rely on signposts when giving directions, so much as we do on landmarks. Actually, you wouldn't want to be relying too heavily on Irish signposts at the best of times. They are notoriously, well, wrong. Or absent.

Examine your surroundings. Is there an old river course that's maybe gone underground? Any wells or springs? Features of glaciation, such as truncated spurs or erratically deposited boulders? If you live in a city or town, are there any trees near you? A park? Any bodies of water within reach? What was the area like before it was built on? The natural features in your locality and the lay of the surrounding land all tell a story. Learn to listen to it. Look at the history of the house you live in, the ground it stands directly on, the people that surround you. Find out all you can by research, first and foremost.

Then you can spend some time, quietly, letting yourself travel into the atmosphere of your own dwelling place. The object of all this is to root you in your home, to help you feel as comfortable as possible in the place you spend the most time, to find out as much as possible about it and what has gone on there in the past. If you don't feel comfortable in your actual house for some reason, if you don't want to connect to where you are living, then the question would be why? How can you make it more comfortable? Have you tried a house cleansing? This can be done as simply as going top to bottom with a purifying incense, such as a herbal bundle. I don't recommend the classic sage smudge stick, or palo santo wood, due to concerns around both cultural appropriation and over-harvesting which endangers the plants - please find something native to your area that you can easily dry and bundle yourself, if you want to cleanse or purify with smoke. You could also cleanse with a salt water or essential oil spray mist, or with sound; a pure clear tone, such as a bell, is excellent. Whichever method you use, it is the intent that is important, really feeling and focusing on the clearing and cleansing process.

If this is not suitable, then how soon can you move to somewhere you feel you can and should connect to? A stable base is important for successful magic or spirituality, and your home should be your physical place of stability. If you are truly stuck somewhere you don't feel you belong in, for the time being, then travel slightly farther afield and find somewhere within easy reach in which you can feel comfortable and connected.

I found myself adopted into County Roscommon here in Ireland, a long time ago. Once we were there, the next step for me was to figure out exactly what sort of neighbours and even house guests, of the non-corporeal kind, I had ended up with. The circle of mature trees on the land beside my house was where I had earmarked for my magical working and outdoor covenstead, so that was the obvious place to start.

Meeting the Trees

The grove was silent and still at first. The hood of my heavy cloak was raised as I wound my way through the tall grasses and dead branches to the centre of the neglected circle. It felt old; the trees were all mature and fully formed in their power and majesty. I grew silent and still as my surroundings came to life. Sinking to the ground, I absorbed the feelings given out by my new acquaintances. To really connect to a particular tree's energy, it is best to go and find a living example of that tree. Sit under or beside it, place or your hands on it, and breathe slowly and deeply. Visualise yourself open to the exchange of energy; feel it connect and flow as you continue to breathe deeply and steadily. Take note of any feelings you receive, or random images, but don't try to analyse them there and then. Acknowledge them, then refocus on your breathing. When you feel finished, thank the tree, and gently break the connection by removing your hands.

In that grove, the trees remain - though my family has since moved on. There is elder, grown taller than any I have seen, glorious in their gnarled antiquity. They are the guardians of the grove and what was then my home. There is hawthorn, carrying the promise of magic and fertility, love and joy, succour and sustenance through the pains of life. The ash stands graceful and proud, with intricate depth and height to explore; they span the bridges of the Universe. Their promise is one of connection and knowledge, gained through sacrifice and commitment. These images came to me through connection with those trees. Their spirits are unique, but part of that grove and the landscape. If you dip a little deeper than the tree itself, you can feel the pulse of the land. After a quiet and restful interlude with the trees that day, so long ago now, I sent them my thanks and respect, rose to my feet, and made my careful way back out of their presence. Even as I entered my back door, I could feel their sighing protection embrace the boundaries of the land around my home with their strength and wisdom.

Meeting the Sidhe

Na Daoine Sidhe are a different matter. The natural elements of a place such as its trees, water, or stones are pretty constant and fairly easy going on the whole. They offer accessible and often uncomplicated journeys and help to the seeker. Not so with the Fairy folk: they are something that must never be taken for granted. Our experiences with the local element here have pretty much all involved protection and pact-making... you certainly need to stay on your toes when working with such beings, whether you believe they love you or hate you. It is possible to work with them and gain from the experience, if you are clever and quick. Having suffered their interest for a time now, I can't in truth say whether I would not prefer to be ignored by their kind. But things are as they are.

The Sidhe are different to us - seems to be stating the obvious I know, but you would be surprised how many folks come to deal with these beings and expect them to play fair by our human standards or morals. They are not human. A lot of them don't have any idea of humans, our world or our rules. They exist on different levels and although they (or we) can cross over between our world and theirs, I don't believe they can do so in any corporeal form. Though in fairness, the theories on that question are many and varied, and the native tradition is often contradictory! The most fundamental form of Fairies are elemental energies and *genus locii* (spirits of a certain place). Not everyone will even agree they are part of the Sidhe as such - though they are residents of the Otherworld, as well as this world. They are often curious about our physical form and the workings of human bodies, and will sometimes try to catch on to us, if we let this happen. This can be detrimental, and if it happens and they are being fed, it is often difficult to convince them to go back to the realms from whence they came!

Not all Sidhe are out to get us, and there are some stories of them being helpful to humans for sure. The majority though would seem to us to have a very malicious - and even vicious - streak in their nature, but I have always found that this is just that: their nature, differences that we perhaps simply don't understand. They are often found around ancient and sacred sites, some of which may well have been built or boundaried specifically due to their gateway function between the worlds. When working with the sites, I can only offer to share some of my own findings. Each place is unique, each energy quite different, and the following will only give you a general guide. Be careful, be sensible, be respectful. Trust your instincts. Have patience and mind your manners. As you learned from meeting the trees, and from the chapter on Folk and Fairies, feel the energy that is around you, but be careful and respectful!

If there are no Raths or Ringforts near where you live, and you don't feel it is practical to go and visit an ancient site with any regularity, then even city parks, havens of nature in the midst of the concrete, may have something to offer. Truly, though, to find the spirits of the land, and the travellers between worlds, you need to look for them in their own environment, not expect them to come to yours. Seek the Sidhe or spirits of your land in the wild and ancient places.

Meeting the Gods

If that is a little on working with natural and the more super-natural elements of the land, then what of its Gods? What role do they play in the integration of a modern Witch with this land? What of the role of Priest or Priestess to one specific God or Goddess?

When looking to make a personal connection with an Irish deity, the obvious thing to do is to come to Ireland. Visit and spend some time at the places that are historically or traditionally connected to that deity. I know I keep saying that, but there is truly no better way to connect to Ireland than to come here. It is not going to be an easy thing to do for many of you. Even for those of us in Ireland, getting to visit the sites while working around our everyday life, or spending any significant amount of time at them, isn't going to be a thing we can practically do on a very regular basis, unless they're pretty close to where you live. That's fair enough. But it does not need to be, at the very least, a long-term goal if at all possible. The full power of this land is at its most potent when felt directly.

All of that being said... I do understand that for some folk, physically being here is just not possible in this lifetime, for a myriad of reasons ranging from disability to economic issues to responsibilities. If that is your situation, don't despair! I have devoted my life to facilitating authentic connection to Ireland, in this world or the Other. I urge you to begin a Journeying practice (there are multiple free and paid options on my YouTube Channel and through the Irish Pagan School, as well as regular resources when you join my mailing list community at https://LoraOBrien.ie), and do your best with what you have.

It is definitely possible to begin working on a connection from elsewhere, right now. Geographical location is not the only important thing:, how you live your life and respect your heritage, and the native culture, are a huge part of this whole big picture too. What you do each day, and how you feel, can be just as important as where you are. If you live in the United States or Australia or Britain or Canada (or anywhere!), and yet feel a strong pull toward this place and its powers… but you can't get here to live or even visit, what can you do?

Start to Learn Irish

My first point of contact would be the language. It is difficult to learn any new language, yes, especially when your culture is anglo-centric or monolingual. But not to make at least an effort with something as basically essential as the language, when you profess to be interested in Irish Witchcraft or Irish Paganism, is verging on the ridiculous. As I have pointed out previously, the language is the heart of any people, and by direct transference: speaking from the heart of the people paves the way to the ears of their Gods. To continually address the Irish Gods in the tongue of their oppressors, with no knowledge of or reference to their own tongue and the heart of their own people, is at best rude and ignorant, and at worst can even be dangerous (depending on a number of other factors). It is not the case that they don't understand English, of course they do, and they can feel what is in the heart of the seeker.

It is respectful to them though, when I greet them in their own tongue, and for me to converse as much as possible in (as close as I can get to) their own native language. It shows that I care. It shows that I am trying to make them comfortable, facilitate them to a certain degree, instead of barging in and smashing around the place with hobnail boots. I am the tourist in their realms, the guest, and I have no desire to be the kind of tourist who expects the native dwellers to speak my language, and feels they're savages if they do not.

That's Colonialism, Chad.

I am not a fluent Irish speaker, though I am improving all the time with regular use. I speak modern Irish and unfortunately have no knowledge of *Sean-Ghaeilge* (Old Irish, a different language really), which would be the language of the people at the time these Gods were first predominant. We think. But I have found that using as much Irish as I can, as often as I can, in ritual and when dealing with the locals on their own sites and ancient places, gives me a certain amount of respect from them in return. And indeed, for those who are tuned in enough to listen to and hear the Sidhe or the local entities at their own places, they will often speak in Irish just to confuse you! This has happened to me while giving guided tours of the sacred sites on many, many occasions. So, start to learn the Irish language (Gaeilge). There are many online resources that will get you started, and then clubs or online groups dedicated to the language worldwide, to further improve. Libraries often have programmes in book and/or CD or DVD form to borrow, or information about where to access the clubs and facilities that might be in your area. (Check the Resources at the end of this book too!)

Study Deity through Myth and Legends

Read everything you can lay your hands on about the God or Goddess you feel a draw to, from academic research and theories to the people who also feel a draw through their Internet sites, books, or poetry on the subject, stories, and tales, children's books, if and how they survive in modern times, and in what form or context (for example, as Saints, in place names, through local tales or traditions, commemorative art or statuary).

Learn too about the history and culture into which these Gods were born, especially if you are not native to it yourself. I include here modern culture and artistic expression, satire, politics and news. All of this is important to understand the core of the deity, because (I believe that) they are in a symbiotic relationship with their people.

Put Out a Call

This is very simple: Find an appropriate place, an appropriate time and call the name of the deity you wish to contact. Introduce yourself. Express your interest. Make no commitment at this stage. It is a suitable time for mutual recognition and greeting, nothing more.

Then, do it again. Show up consistently.

Wait

Armed with your background knowledge and information – and this study, if done in full earnestness, will not just take a few Google searches and a flip through the local library or bookshop's Irish fairy tales collection – the next step is to wait. Yes, you wait. And you watch. And you listen.

No barging in half-cocked to summon the deity to your presence and offer yourself wholeheartedly into their service, please. Through the knowledge you have gained, you may start to see signs filtering into your life, seemingly at random. They may come as dreams, as physical happenings that could be seen as omens, things that happen in the mundane that immediately remind you of the deity, or a tale connected to them. Or they may just happen as a seemingly disconnected series of coincidences. During this waiting period, be as honest with yourself as you can manage. Does stepping in a pile of dog poo really indicate that Crom Cruach, the great recycler, has chosen you? Or is it just a pile of dog poo? When your kitchen goes on fire, does it really mean that Brighid, Goddess of the flame, wants you to personally tend her hearth? Or did you just leave the matches within easy reach of your 4 year old? The line between destructive self-doubt and healthy self-examination is often a wobbly one, especially when you are new to all this and the supernatural is so different to you from the natural. We have to try though.

This is where a daily record of this time will prove invaluable. In a journal, preferably, record what you see, what you feel, your dreams, the phases and cycles in your life or of the sun/moon, and what strikes you as odd or appropriate throughout your day. But reserve judgement or conclusion until your waiting period has passed. Just observe, write it down, and go on to the next day. A suitable time frame would be anything from one moon cycle (28 days in full), to one season (marked from one seasonal celebration day to the next), to your full term as *Cuairteoir* (a year and a day, at least... see the chapter on Stages of a Witch's Life for more on this). How long you wait will depend on your own development previous to this. Generally speaking, the newer you are to magic and spirituality, the longer you should wait before making any sort of formal commitment to a particular path/tradition, or to any specific God or Goddess.

Again, be patient, and be honest with yourself. Question yourself often, and really think about your answers. Record them. They will change over time. As you look back through your journal you will see patterns, some certainties forming, some seemingly random occurrences that happen far too often or too intensely to be truly called random. Pay attention.

Why?

What I have described thus far can be used by anybody who wishes to connect to a particular God or Goddess energy, to bring some of that power into their lives. If after your connection and waiting period you decide truly and honestly that the chosen God or Goddess has responded - or called to you in some way - and you wish to proceed with the dedication process... that is when the real work must begin.

Yes, it is complicated. Yes, it is hard work. Yes, it will take a lot of your time and effort and energy. If you are one of those who couldn't be bothered, fair enough. Maybe at some stage, you will be. Maybe you won't. It's not for everyone – and to be perfectly honest with you, Dear Reader, dedicating yourself to a particular deity can often be more trouble than it's worth, in the sense of your own gain or advancement. Much of the work I find myself doing in the grand scheme of things is altruistic at best, and most of the time is just plain thankless. In short, having a God on your side might seem like the ultimate power trip, but it puts you squarely as a willing pawn on a very vast chessboard. It won't make you popular, it won't make you rich, and it certainly won't make you happy – it will usually just lead to you doing more work.

So why do it? Why would you want to dedicate yourself to a deity?

A lot of folk find they don't have much choice. They find themselves led by the nose; circumstance twisting and turning them in a particular direction until it's pretty much unavoidable. For those who actually want it… oh all right, it's not always as bleak as all that. Even those who are plucked by the ear and led to a particular God or Goddess do gain from the experience. Personal growth is the main gain, self-knowledge, and magical experience. That is, of course, as much from the sheer amount of work you need to put in on a practical level to gain access to their realms and their presence, as from any particular favours or insights bestowed by them. And I must admit, putting aside for the moment the grumpy old grouch hat that I don at times… the feeling and experience of connection with a divine being is an amazing and awesome one to have (in the literal 'awe-inspiring' sense of the word). It'll knock your socks off. It is beautiful, terrifying, inspiring, driving, and wondrous – inexplicable really, but that's as close as I can get. To touch that power, to feel its flow going both ways, to be that close to the Source, that's what makes all the toil and hardship worthwhile. It sounds idealistic and romanticised, I know, and the skeptics among you will be scoffing right now. Scoff away, skeptics! Until you touch it personally, it is idealistic and romanticised. And then it's real. And the deity is real, and it manifests in your life in a hundred different ways. The longer you continue the relationship, the more you see God on a daily basis and are comforted, strengthened, and upheld by that presence. And that's why we do it.

Or, one of the main reasons why I do it, at least.

If that's why we do it, then the obvious next question is **how** do we do it?

[You can get a much fuller picture of all of this in my other book, 'A Practical Guide to Pagan Priesthood' (Llewellyn, 2019), which I recommend you read before making any sort of deity commitment - or indeed, before joining any group, so you'll know what to reasonably expected from the Priesthood running it!]

Go and Visit

From your research and study, you will be quite familiar with the places, traits, and things that are associated with your chosen deity. For Brighid it could be flame or iron wrought by a smith; for the Dagda, it might be a harp, a club, or a cauldron; for Bóann, the river Boyne or cow symbolism; and for the Mórrígan, it might be blood, caves, or crows. You get the idea.

If you can, of course, you should come to their special places physically. If you cannot, a spiritual or psychic journey is necessary, preferably while geographically located somewhere resembling their special places (for example, if you can't get to *Uaimh na gCat* to say hello in person to the Mórrígan, then try and find another cave). The idea is that any cave is better than no cave, and all caves are possible links to the Otherworld in essence.

If this is strictly impossible (and not just inconvenient; bear in mind that there are very few people who genuinely can't manage at least the occasionally day trip if there is a site within a reasonable distance), then it will be necessary to construct a non corporeal site. Get as many pictures and reports of the place you wish to visit as you can find and literally build - over a series of meditations, visualisations, and Journeys - the place in your mind. You do this until you can see it all clearly, hold it easily, smell the earth and surroundings, hear the sounds, taste the air, and touch every rock and blade of grass. The technique is similar to the 'building your astral temple' or 'creating your sacred space' instructions given in so many modern magical how-to books – which this book is not. You can however access a whole lot of very practical Journeying support and learning over at the Irish Pagan School.

All of this will usually, unless you are particularly accomplished with these techniques already, take quite a time and be an exercise in tuning into the deity's and the land's energy in itself. Even if you have a handy cave or passage grave tomb that you can physically be in, do not bypass this psychic and energetic build-up if it is not the actual place that is associated with your chosen deity. You still need to tune in.

If you have access to the specific location you wish to be in, then a series of visits will be necessary, again to tune in. Once there, you will also need to be able to go into a trance state easily. Only by continuous regular practice will this be possible. A countdown or mental journey downward (descending steps works well), inward, or upward - depending on your practice! - will be necessary to lead you in to the magical atmosphere of the place, as well as being physically located there. And be sure you are quite comfortable with getting back out again.

Marian Green covers a lot of these techniques in her books on magic, and as I mentioned I have done a whole lot to create resources for Guided Journeying in the Irish Otherworld. And really, if you are not at least familiar with this sort of magical work already, what the heck are you doing dedicating yourself to a deity? Do you have any idea what you are letting yourself in for? Go back and stick with the first few steps outlined here, and keep working on your magical development before you make such an intense commitment.

What's your hurry?

Ritual Dedication

Some sort of simple ritual or dedication, something practical, may be a necessary part of this process for you. It can be done before, after, or during the psychic Journey you are making. Switching from internal to external work (the physical elements of setting up and performing a ritual) can often be a good thing. It confuses you slightly, brings you harshly from one world to the next, making you a 'walker between the worlds'. The physical ritual will tune your conscious mind, as well as the subconscious, to the work at hand. It can be very simple.

An offering to the deity is a good place to start, followed by your statement of intent, a formal dedication if you wish to do so, a bit of a praise poem or prayer never goes amiss, a talismanic link to them that you can charge and then carry afterward, and some food and drink for when you are finished.

I am sure I do not need to remind the folks who are visiting actual ancient or natural sites that nothing you do should leave **any** trace at that place. No candle wax, no hot tea lights placed on stones (they can crack and split), no crystals left in cracks or buried, no bonfires, no rubbish, no ridiculous bits of plastic or anything else tied to the poor trees. Your offering, if left there, should be completely biodegradable; and quickly at that. If in a cave, for example, bear in mind that your bit of apple will not rot down for a very long time, and is just rubbish and clutter. If somebody visited your home would you be grateful if they left rotting fruit or plastic bags tied around the place? I think not.

As to what to use for an offering, the matter is very delicate. Use your common sense, and leave nothing destructive or unsightly. It should be something that means something to you, and something of a sacrifice can work well - a thing you will feel the loss of on some level. If you want to establish a very personal connection to the site - and think carefully about the possible repercussions of that, it's a two-way street! - some of your own hair is usually appropriate, or some of your own blood. Or you can use something that can be burned without causing any damage and released that way, instead of left to rot slowly. Plan this carefully or you will get somebody local who may be a bit grumpy in their site guardianship (such as me, I do this) who comes along and, without compunction, removes your carefully placed item from the site and throws it away as the rubbish it has become, without a second thought.

State Your Intent

Your statement of intent is probably best done before you go inwards, openly, and as formally or as simply as you like. It can be anything from you saying, 'I am here to dedicate myself to [insert deity name here]'... to a full-blown track record of your ancestry and origins, how you came to be in that particular place at that particular time, or anything that feels like it should be said. Perhaps it is best to plan it simply, with the basics, and expand or ad lib as when you feel it is right or fitting.

Descend

Once you are in and attuned, you can sit and wait for the deity to contact you, or call them, or do your dedication then and there. This can be like any other contractual arrangement: you make it clear what you are offering to their service, and what you come to this arrangement bearing as your gifts or your treasures. You also should have an idea of what you want in return from the deity. I find when working with Gods, especially the Irish ones, that given half a chance they will take you for all they can get. They also don't seem to want or respect grovelling or subservience, in my personal experience. They come from a time of warriors; men and women alike. It is important to remember that it was only in the 600s CE that Adomnan, the Abbot of Iona, formulated the rule that exempted women from military service. Women were often just as fierce as their menfolk, perhaps more so if they had children and homes to directly protect, and this is shown amply by the likes of Scathach (the warrior woman who trained Cú Chulainn), Bodhmall the Druid (Fionn Mac Cumhaill's aunt, who raised him) and her female partner Liath Luachra the Warrior... and by the fact that the Irish Gods of war are actually Goddesses. Strength, bravery, and courage are respected and expected. Anybody who has faced the wrath of a typical Irish Mammy (and lived to tell the tale) will bear witness to the truth of this, even today.

This is not to say that there is no place for healthy respect and even fear; those who do not fear such powers as that wielded by the Gods are foolish. I think 'feel the fear and do it anyway' is as good a motto here as it is in any other working, whether it be magical or mundane.

How I Went About Things

Many modern Witches have a huge interest in the Mórrígan. She is the Witch of the Tuatha Dé Danann, known as one of the most powerful entities in the Irish pantheon. She is a shape-shifter, a dark being who is often mentioned in the tales, but whose contradictions are little explained.

Living where I did, she held an obvious attraction for me. And realistically, she is probably the main reason I ended up living where I did for so many years. Roscommon is still something of a hidden county, where, unless you are into the scholarly study of Irish myths and legends (which I subsequently came to, thankfully); you perhaps would not associate with anything magical. It was just someplace you would pass through on your way to the West of Ireland.

Whenever I told anybody I was moving there, the response was always, "Roscommon, where's that then? On the way to Mayo?" I still can't quite believe I wasted so much time all those years hanging around Newgrange and the usual tourist places, when this undiscovered and untapped majesty was right here, with very few left to work it. Newgrange is great and all, but there's so much more to spiritual Ireland than that!

Once the offer on the house I was buying there was in and accepted, and it was set that I was going to be living in Roscommon for a time at least, I started to do some research. I nearly fell over myself when I discovered that *Ráth Cruachán* (Rathcroghan), the court of Connacht Queen Medb (Maeve) and her consort King Ailill Mac Mata, was just 10 minutes from my new house. As if that wasn't enough, there was also *Uaimh na gCat* (pron. Ooav nah Goth), the 'Cave of the Cats'; entrance to the Otherworld, and the Mórrígan's "fit abode". That is where she resides. That is the place historically that she comes from and goes to. That, I felt, was the place from which her ancient priestesses worked their magic and mysteries in her honour and service, through time.

That was where I would make contact with a Goddess.

A Note for the 2nd Edition:

In the first edition of this book, I took a number of experiences I had around that time, and amalgamated them into a cohesive story of my meeting of the Mórrígan. None of it was untrue, in any way, but it didn't happen all together like I felt I had to present at that time - partly for the sake of my own youthful pride, if I'm completely honest - but mostly for the privacy of my family, and of the people I working magically and spiritually with, as well as pressure I was under in my relationship, at that time.

I've made things a little clearer, slightly less personal, and hopefully more practically useful for my readers, in the slight re-writing and clarification of this next section, while still staying true to the original edition as much as possible.

Step 1: Go and Visit

I avoided her caves for more than a year. I meant to go down, hundreds of times I said to myself, "Tonight, I can go to the cave tonight". I visited friends, as their home is near the entrance and they had offered to take care of my girls while I climbed down. I meant to go down, so many times. But something always happened, something always came up, something always got in the way.

Journeying to darkness is not as simple as it is at times made out to be. Some folk would have you believe that meditating on a crow feather or a scrap of blood on some tissue is enough for you to 'meet the dark ones', and then you can go on about your business in the usual fashion. This sort of thing can be a start, an introduction perhaps, but it certainly is not the end or all of the experience. Whatever we take on while in the Otherworld, manifests in this world. To start on this path can be the spiritual equivalent of taking a 6-foot staff and thudding on the massive oaken door of the Universe, with the mad cry of, "Hey you, here I am! Bring it on", reverberating through the expanse of time and space. The Universe looks out its little spy hole at you standing there in all your glorious door-thudding insanity, and says, "Oh, it's you is it. You want it? Fasten your seat-belt matey, coz here we go".

I mean, that's not literally how it happens, but you get me.

The ways in which the Universe chooses to manifest itself, and your Journey through the necessary darkness in your life, are many and varied. It can be about facing your own fears, through self-examination and soul-searching. It can be about finally learning the lessons that occur and re-occur in our lives, through our mistakes and our life choices. It can be about dealing with death and pain, about picking yourself up after a fall or a knockdown and getting on with it, assimilating the lesson in that. It can be about releasing your own demons, walking into the madness of your own soul and crawling out the other side. If you go the route of picking a fight - again, not literally, please - with a specific deity, then the *craic* really starts. You get all the above, plus the fun and games of having a strong personality front on the Universe – with all its care and attention focused right on little old you.

The Mórrígan has always fully fascinated and truly terrified me. She is a Goddess of great power and fear, great strength and potency, great honesty and hunger. She can be as nasty as a bed of snakes, or as toweringly tremendous as a hurricane. She is not a force to be trifled with, and I was quite happy to shy away from her intricacies and play quietly in the sunshine of my innocence. Unfortunately for me – or perhaps, fortunately, in the grand scheme of things – she had other ideas.

It all started with the move to Roscommon, I see that now.

Well, of course, it started a long time before that; the Irish Gods had taken my initial stubborn clinging to the light 'n fluffies of my Baby Paganism as something of a challenge, and started to chuck stuff at me. I had been initiated into a Wiccan coven at that stage, too, and initiations of any sort are practically guaranteed to throw your life into some sort of turmoil. My mistake was believing I was somehow safe while dealing with the Craft and my own inner path walking. I'd been trying to unobtrusively hug the curtains at the party that was my life, attempting desperately to stay in the corner, unobserved and unnoticed (so I thought) while I tried to sort my own shit out. But, I know now I was naive, and I'd already come to the attention of the Gods, somehow.

Maybe the initiations had something to do with it, in hindsight?!

Over time, I found a semblance of balance and belief – both in myself and in the forces that guided and led me in that move to Roscommon. I read all I could find about the history and archaeology of the sites, about the mythology of the area, about the cycles and legends and epics that concerned my new home. This was all part of my own 'Go and Visit' period.

At this point in time, I honestly don't remember which was the **very** first time I went in to the Mórrígan's Cave. Tourists visit there regularly, then and now - they troupe down in the mud and the grime and the darkness, then they clamber back up and out into the light and go home again. Most are none the wiser for their slice of Ireland; it is just another site, another check off their list of things to do. Some are disconcerted when they emerge, some are relieved, some can sense the curtain that is usually kept tightly closed in the places of power. Some few even feel they could reach out and lift it aside, see what is beyond the Veil, even step through... if only they dared. I knew (in theory) what was there; I could feel it in my dreams and on my visits to the sites of *Cruachán*. Over time, I came to understand that my relationship with the Cave was leading to a commitment, to something. I did not understand that it would be a commitment to her specifically, just... to something. What I didn't know was what would happen to me once I made that commitment.

I brewed the knowledge that I gained about the caves and the Rathcroghan area, turned it over and over in my mind until it crystallised into jewels of ideas, nuggets of knowledge to be stored and utilised when I needed them. I stewed on the feelings that rose in my breast at the mention of the Mórrígan; the emotions and depth of knowing that were churned up inside me each time a crow cawed, each time I dreamed of her shifting shadow, each time I acknowledge the strength of the fear that stirred in me at the mere mention of her name.

The first time I went to the Cave in desperation, seeking aid for a specific situation (which I thought at the time would come from the Tuatha Dé Danann generally, through the Otherworld entrance... maybe Dian Cécht the Healer would help?), it was the Mórrígan that showed up. I was not expecting her to be interested in a healing circumstance, but as I said - I was desperate. In that moment, in that space, a commitment was made. I got what I needed, and I agreed to work for her.

I do not recommend going about things that way though, so I will now turn you to what happened after that, which is more usual, and generally useful to those of you reading here.

From that point, she seemed to be everywhere in my life. I don't think I had fully resigned or aligned myself to what I had agreed to in the Cave, but she was calling me to do her work, and there is no getting away from that call. Everywhere I turned, I was reminded of her. The crows surrounded my home in their hundreds; every day they shouted at me. Her voice echoed in my dreams, in strange snatches of dread and desire. I flew with those crows on their wheeling wondrous flights through the expanse of the skies (and still do), in dreams and visions and Journeys. My days were interlaced with longing and life, my nights with dread and death. Every day, in every way, she called.

And all the time it grew, the commitment I had made loomed large in my life. She was calling me, commanding me, for her own reasons. The following Samhain, I decided I had had enough of all that, and wanted to take some control of the situation, I think? So, I decided to dedicate myself formally, and step into it wholeheartedly.

Step 2: Ritual Dedication

A simple ceremony sounded good. I had made the choice, I knew what I had to do, and it was time. What was it I suggested? 'An offering to the God or Goddess is a good start, then a formal dedication and your statement of intent, a talismanic link to them that you can change and then carry afterward, and some food and drink for when you are finished'. That sounds good. It sounds simple enough. What did I do?

97

Tattoos. My dedication to herself came when a Pagan tattooist friend of mine offered to make my crow design a reality, then and there, on a quiet day in my tattoo and body piercing shop (the business I was running at the time - I was the body piercer). It wasn't planned, it wasn't even fully understood at the time, but this was my first test, my dedication. I carry 29 crows with me from that day, everywhere I go. (More have been added since, but that's a story for another day.) They are my talismanic link to her. They have taught me that the Mórrígan will not take your pain away, but she can help you deal with it and become all the stronger for it. After letting that sink in for quite a while, I felt I was ready.

Step 3: State your Intent

After seeking the practical advice of a respected local guide, I made my way to the entrance of *Uaimh na gCat*: the entrance to the Otherworld. I wasn't alone. Two other women were called and willing to make the assay on the same night. We had made a lot of preparations prior to the night, and once outside it was time to state our intent. But none of us really knew why we were there. We recognised the need to be there, but not the purpose. I thought it might have something to do with becoming her Priestess. I tried so hard to convince myself that this was alright, that I would be okay and safe and not dead when all this was said and done. In the end, we settled on the bonds of sisterhood as our common purpose – although each would descend alone, each was connected and an aid to the others. It was time.

Step 4: Descend

The description that follows is that of my genuine experiences, but it is not complete. The full account of what happened at various times and various visits to those caves was given by me, committed to computer memory, and subsequently (without any logical explanation) wiped from that memory – as if it had never been. I hadn't been sure to what extent I should go into my experiences with herself. I wanted to get it all down and decide afterward what I should and should not use for the book, but that experience told me I had gone into too much. So what follows is my second attempt to give you, Dear Reader, as full as possible an account, without betraying the mysteries of the initiations or the trials that I, and others alongside me, have gone through at this place. As mentioned above, it is something of an amalgamation of various times, but if it feels incomplete to you, now you know why. I can only offer my apologies – but you must realise, and I hope respect, that my loyalties lie with herself, and with my sisters.

The access tunnel is man-made. The rough stone walls were damp and slimy as I slid and slipped on my back, down into the muddy blackness below. There is a T-junction about 6 or 7 feet in. To the right lies a hollowed-out alcove just big enough to sit in, and to the left, the tunnel leads down about 25 feet to the natural cave entrance. The floor is thick mud and large rocks, the walls are slick, and the air is cool and still. After initially trying to pick my way through the inches-deep mud at the entrance, I gave up on trying to keep clean and just slid on my arse down to the shelf that marks the natural cave beginning. I figured I might as well surrender myself to the experience completely. Embrace the mud.

As I broke through to the cavern beyond, I turned off the torch I had thought to bring. If I was embracing the mud, I might as well go the whole hog and embrace the darkness. I gave a quick flick to get the lay of the land: took in the way the floor dips in the centre and then rises towards the roof at the far end, the way the calcium carbonate turned the walls a weird white hue in the soft gleam of the torch, the water dripping through from the land that lay above, the roof's climb to the apex at about 20 feet above, and its gradual descent to meet the floor high up on the other end. As I resolutely switched off my only light and continued my descent into this womb of the earth, I carefully swallowed my longing to turn around, turn on the torch, and turn my destiny from this dank and deathly place. I kept my slippery slide headed for the centre of the cave floor. As I reached what I roughly deemed to be the middle ground in the cavern, the panic and bile rose so suddenly in my throat that I had an incredibly tough time not screaming and running away. Long slow breaths calmed the natural reflex of removing myself from what every sense was telling me to be a dangerous situation. Fight or flight, isn't that what they say your choices are... or freeze? I stayed where I was, stood straight in the darkness and continued to breathe deeply while I gathered myself for battle.

Eyes open or closed, it made no difference. The darkness was complete, a living thing in itself that mirrored my breaths in its void. I listened. The silence listened back. The walls around me felt like a physical body, with life coursing through it in the form of energy and power flow. I stood, silent and alone, in the receptacle of the Otherworld.

As I got my bearings, and the deep breathing worked to calm and centre me, I took myself into my trance state. Physically taking myself down had been the first step; doing it magically must come next. The cave took on even greater depth and levels of intensity as I turned myself around to sense the power spot, to feel the way in, to figure out where to gain access and audience. I felt it to be at the top end. That was where the heavy stage curtain lay thick and twitching with Otherworldly life and energies behind it. On this initial foray, it didn't feel it right or proper to go and pull that curtain aside on my own authority. So I called to them, the guides and guardians of this place – her personnel if you like, those who prepared the way, vetted the worthy from the unworthy, and guided both the wary and the unwary. I was made aware of a line of priesthood, stretching through the ages, in and around this physical place.

The darkness of the caves and the mysteries of the darkness had lain primarily with the women to attend. These were my spiritual ancestors, connected by choice. There were male presences also, but the feeling I got was that she finds all those who identify as women interesting and useful. They all have their cycle to offer. This does not just include the fertile few who bleed monthly. It encompasses the entire spectrum of experience with those cycles – from the barren to the broken, from cis to trans, from the development of sexuality to fertility, to the loss of any cycle in any woman's lifetime. The men were different... some had come, and still do come, to serve and gain there. Some she has no time for; they mean nothing to her. Some have unique gifts to offer, and all have their own powers, their own challenges for the application and use of that power. In that particular place, in that particular way, though, only specific men were found to be interesting or useful. At least, that has been my understanding and experience.

All that being said, I met three guides - none of whom I expected to see. Only one was a priestess of old. The other two were male figures who had something particular to teach me. I listened and learned and thanked them all for their input and help. And then it was time – the exchanging of vows.

As I intoned her name, I was guided into a specific pronunciation, particular inflection, and the proper form of address for her became crystal clear to me: *Mór Ríon*. Great Queen. Once I had it, it vibrated of its own accord through the still air, with the cavern acting as a natural sound chamber to amplify and resonate the call, reaching through the curtain and formally inviting herself to my presence. There were surprising insights given, none of which made sense to me at the time. A connection with Crom Cruach, a truly ancient God of this land. I balked at the brute masculinity, but realised darkness is darkness, and the Mórrígan is older than her name and not bound by our perceptions of gender; she represents in her modem form a power more ancient than speech, more ancient than titles, an integral part of what humans are and what we face, as a race and as a people.

She came to me, stayed apart from me, and we spoke. It was a circling of combatants more than a cosy welcoming chat, I must admit. She was strong and proud. She asked for my commitments, what she wanted from me. Some of it I agreed to gladly, some of it I would not or could not commit. My life became hers, my work for her, but I could not commit anything that was not mine to give. In return, she agreed to my requests, with the acknowledgment of more to come, in an ongoing 'you scratch my back and I'll scratch yours' sort of arrangement. Some of it I do not remember, though it was clear as day at the time. Once I re-entered the light it was lost to my conscious mind, but I presume my subconscious has retained it and has been working away as it must, all this time.

A lot of what occurred, both at the time and since, I cannot reveal. The revelations' I have laid out may seem slight, and they may be disagreed with. Everything I have written about her, I feel, are points that need to be addressed and made public. At the end of the day, as far as I am concerned, a connection was made. Oaths were sworn, from both parties. My life is better and I am stronger for it. Perhaps she is, too.

And sure, isn't that the point of any of this?

5

Cycle and Sabbats

The Sabbats as modern Witches and Pagans celebrate them are commonly called the Wheel of the Year, and consist of eight main seasonal festivals spread throughout the calendar year. You will often see them laid out as follows:

- Yule, Winter Solstice, Midwinter: December 20, 21, or 22
- Imbolg, Candlemas, Imbolc, or Brigid's Day: February 1 or 2
- Eostar, Spring Equinox, Ostara, or Oestarra: March 20, 21, or 22
- Beltane, May Eve, Beltaine, Bealtaine, or May Day: April 30 to May 1
- Litha, Summer Solstice, or Midsummer: June 20, 21, or 22
- Lúnasa, Lughnasa, Lughnasadh, or Lammas: August 1 or 2
- Mabon, Autumn/Fall Equinox, or Harvest Home: September 20, 21, or 22
- Samhain, All Hallow's Eve, Hallowmas: October 31 to November 1

Some of the names and association that have creeped into these festivals are just plain wrong, made up Neo-Pagan bullshit (I'm looking at you, Ostara and Mabon), but that's a little outside the scope of this book. There's plenty of information about this on the internet now we're into the second edition here, thankfully. And some of them just draw directly from Irish (or other 'Celtic') sources - as well as a few other cultures - mixing the traditions into a jumbled, culturally appropriated mess. But when we know better, we can do better. Going forward, I'd like us to do better?

In Ireland, the festivals are divided into two groupings: the Fire festivals, and the Solar festivals. Post christianity, Irish people mainly celebrated the Fire festivals as they form a cohesive and relevant cycle alone, speaking in both practical and mythological terms, so these also became our more recent community folk festivals too. They would probably not have bothered about direct dates specifically, going rather by the times of each year when certain things happened, such as the lambing, the harvests, and other easily marked events. Indeed, originally, there were only two main themes to the year that we can historically distinguish: warm Summertime and cold Wintertime. These times were known as *Sam* (Summer period) and *Gam* (Winter period), in Old Irish. They may have been associated with periods of work and rest, light and dark, or any other opposing/balancing forces. Within these two main times, there came two more divisions with the onset of early farming – those we now know as Spring and Autumn. These four Irish 'Quarter Day' festivals are what we know as the Fire festivals. They are as follows:

- Samhain (pron. SOW-when, generally) - October 31st. Also known as Hallowe'en, All Hallow's Eve. Generally considered the Witch's New Year.
- Imbolg (pron. Ih-Mull-g) - February 1st or 2nd. Also known as Candlemas, Oimelc, Imbolc, and St. Brigid's Day in Ireland.
- Bealtaine (pron. Bee-OWL-tinna) - April 30th. Also known as Beltane (anglicised version), May Eve, Walpurgis Night, Rood mass.
- Lúnasa (pron. LOO-nah-Sah) - August 1st or 2nd. Also known as Lammas Eve, August Eve, Lady Day Eve.

The dates I give for Samhain and Bealtaine are the eves, the evening before, as it is the turning point itself that is especially celebrated at these times. Imbolg and Lúnasa are usually celebrated on the day and are all day... but also continue through the season. You will see different dates given for these Sabbats or festivals in different sources; I have chosen the ones I have because they are the ones that make sense to me personally. The exact date isn't specifically important; it is the spirit of the season that matters most. Some folks don't even go by dates, preferring the method of following or noticing events in their own calendar that make sense in conjunction with the spirit of the festival, and celebrating then. I use dates, though they are often flexible, mainly for simplicity's sake. I don't think my former coven would have appreciated too much being informed that they would be summoned for Imbolg when I saw the first snowflake or for Lúnasa when my carrots got big enough to satisfy a hungry rabbit. So, as do most modern Witches, we use the dates for convenience.

I will only deal with the Solstices and Equinoxes briefly here. They are the Solar festivals, but many hold them in high value. And of course, our ancient ancestors absolutely recognised them, as they built entire massive monuments that aligned to them. They are as follows:

- **Winter Solstice, Midwinter;** December 21-22. The date is changeable; it is always the shortest day of the year.
- **Spring Equinox;** March 21-22. The date is changeable; it occurs when day and night are exactly equal.
- **Summer Solstice, Midsummer;** June 21-22. The date is changeable; it is always the longest day of the year.
- **Autumn Equinox;** September 21-22. The date is changeable; it occurs when day and night are exactly equal.

Winter Solstice, or Midwinter, is the only one I will really miss describing to you, Dear Reader. As we don't really do Christmas in our house, Midwinter (sometimes called Yule) is a time for friends and family to gather, a bright light of feasting and festivity shining in the depths of Winter. The others are often repetitions of the themes that are well covered by the Fire festivals, though they can have specific merit in their own right.

It has been suggested to me that the act of basing our yearly celebrations on agricultural sureties is fairly irrelevant in our modern world. I disagree. I do realise that most of us don't wait in hope and malnourishment for the first sheep's milk at Imbolg. Not many of us will strictly be counting on a good and bountiful harvest at Lúnasa to get our family through the lean Winter. Even for those of us who go the route of the smallholder and grow/raise our own food to eat, there is always the shop. We won't starve if the spuds get a blight, the chickens go on strike, or the carrot fly is particularly vicious. So why bother? What relevance does the cycle of the year, as seen through the eyes of our agricultural ancestors, hold for us now?

There is the importance of our ancestral ties, for one. Linking into rites and traditions of those who have gone before is important for us, as a people, for continuity and stability. It is comforting and inspiring to do something that your great-great-great grandmother probably did. Walk the same paths, perform the same actions, and experience the same joy and pain. This is important, but not enough on its own. 'Because it's always been done this way' doesn't hold a lot of meaning for most of us when it's the only reason for doing something. Or at least, it really shouldn't be the only reason for doing anything, ever.

But there are other reasons. I believe that one of the reasons so many people are now turning to the older ways can be seen in how we live our lives today. Modern culture ignores cycles. We see little separation of night and day, Summer and Winter, and there's no time allocated for proper rest periods. We are up before the sun rises and out until after it sets, in quite a lot of cases. We are out of tune with natural ways.

Without getting all New Age on you, natural rhythms and cycles are of vital importance to our spiritual – as well as our physical – well being. The disconnection and isolation that is rife in today's societies can, I feel, be quite squarely blamed for many of the problems of today's societies. (And also capitalism plus toxic patriarchy, but that's definitely outside the scope of this book... find me on Facebook for more like that!) Although the agricultural cycles in themselves were important in times past, I believe that celebrating certain themes at certain times of the year was also important in itself. This is to do with a realisation (perhaps subconscious) that we, as humans, have the need to follow a natural rhythm of some form. Today, we can take the agricultural cycles as still valid, no matter how we fit them to our lives. As you begin or continue to work with the festivals, your life starts to fall into a natural rhythm again.

You gain a greater sense of completion with each year that passes. Tasks become easier, as there is a 'right' time to do certain things. It all happens naturally as it should. Things just start to slowly and inconspicuously fall into place. For example, I don't have to be growing lettuce or onions in order to benefit from the fruits of my labour. Without my planning it as such, the proposal (plan) for this book was accepted by the publisher at Samhain. I have grown it and nurtured it all through the dark of Winter, in order to let it go at Bealtaine, a full-grown manuscript. I will then face the inevitable harvesting around Lúnasa – chopping apart my thoughts and notions in the editing process so we can glean the bounty of greater clarity. The release date is just after Samhain, a full year's cycle of a project which holds every bit as much interest and importance to me and my family as any farmer's crop ever did. This is just one example, of course; there are many such things large and small, that fit into your natural cycle once you are working the Wheel of the Year. And so it begins.

Samhain (October 31st)

This festival was celebrated as a three-day event. It is given in the Coligny calendar as *Trinouxtion Samonii* – which translates roughly as 'Three Nights of the End of Summer'. In modern times its new face of Hallowe'en has grown to a massive event in many countries; even in the UK, where Guy Falkes Night has been predominant, we still see similar themes. Death (murder and sacrifice), fire and light in the darkness (bonfires and fireworks displays), and behind the scenes activity, all remain large parts of the celebration. The feast has been christianised as All Soul's Eve (October 31), which was known as All Hallow's Eve, and All Saint's Day (November 1). Even in such a form, the death theme is prevalent, remembering those who have gone before.

Part of remembering and honouring the past is the theme of remembering our dead. Thoughts turn to death in earnest at this festival, it looms upon us, and this naturally brings about memories of ancestors and those who have already passed through. Many homes in Ireland still lay the 'dumb supper'. This is the placement of one full meal on Samhain night (that is, the 31st), at the family's table. This usually consisted of a dinner in the evening, with an empty chair available, for any passing family or friendly spirits who might drop in. The windows and doors are left unlocked all night (by those who deem it safe to do so; locked doors are an unfortunate factor of this rather less trustworthy world in which we live). These customs are given as a sign of welcome for the ghosts that are about at this time of year. The extra meal is left outside when the family has finished its meal. None of the living may consume the food meant for the dead; it was said that they would be barred from partaking of it after their own death if they were greedy enough to touch it while living. The theme of honouring the dead, and aiding them in any way possible, is very prominent at this festival. Perhaps because of the significant reminder that as we are coming into the time of death, it may be us who pass on before too long. Many would not have survived a hard Winter, and at Samhain, it is usually too early to tell if the weather will turn nasty or the food will run out. There may have been an element of hedging our bets, so to speak, by being polite and utterly respectful to the dead spirits, and the spirits of death, at this time.

Samhain involved the culling of stock; animals that would go towards the store of Winter food and that were surplus to requirements through the Winter (those that were old, past their prime, or the surplus males). It was a necessary and sacrificial slaughter, as keeping them alive would be a drain on the feed stores for the other animals. Though an essential agricultural activity, it would have made sense to use the deaths as a sacrifice to the spirits of the land, in thanks for the harvest and to ensure goodwill for the new year's cycle. The meat was cured and stored as part of the interior or domestic work to come, to provide essential staples to the Winter food for humans. So it was a time of sacrifice and death, but also of cleansing: cutting out the old stock and preparing those remaining for the coming Winter. All around Ireland, the bonfires that symbolised this cleansing and purification are still in evidence and are a part of nearly every community's year. In any modern Irish town still, there will be a Hallowe'en bonfire of some description, though the locals will usually not understand where the importance that is traditionally placed upon this yearly ritual actually stems from. Not consciously, at least!

In the past, all the household fires would be extinguished on Samhain Eve. This in itself is unusual. The morning's fire would have been lit with the embers of the night before, indeed and it still is in many households. A cold hearth was kept all day on Samhain Eve. At Tlachtga, just over 20 km or 12 miles from Tara as the crow flies, the sacred bonfire was relit, with new vigour to see the people through the coming Winter and reaffirm the strength and survival of the people. With the kindling of the new flame, spreading across the land from sacred site to sacred site, thoughts could turn to the new year cycle. The massive bonfires, with the associated feasting and community huddle, also (I suppose) served the purpose of somewhat dispelling the uneasiness that the coming darkness would bring to many a mind, a reminder that strong flame could and would be kindled, even in the depths of the darkness about to descend.

It is often difficult to understand to our modern minds how this festival is given as the 'Celtic New Year', and indeed, we're not completely sure now that this is historically accurate. In modern times, we are imprinted with the thought of new year and new beginnings happening in early Spring. In reality, when examining the cycle of the year, it doesn't make a lot of sense to celebrate the New Year on January 1. Nothing new is really happening; it's still the dead of Winter. And yet the joy, new resolutions, new beginnings that are such an important part of the modern celebration are a reflection of the predilection we still feel for marking the turning cycles and making a considered fresh start.

And yet, with some thought, it becomes clear that all vital growth starts in pure darkness and still silence. The Irish marked the days from dusk to dusk, this we do know – giving due importance to the period of rest and regeneration, the blackness of the night. For example, the human womb protects a new forming life in its secret safety, and all the true formation has taken place by the time we start to see the outward sign of its presence. It is long before the fist or the leg pushes out like some alien creature about to break the skin, that the development of the essential aspects of the foetus are well and truly done. By just 10 weeks old, before most people even realise they are pregnant, the facial features, limbs, hands, feet, finger, and toes of a foetus are formed. Its nervous system is responsive, and many of the internal organs begin to function. All this happens in the dark stillness of the womb.

At Samhain, we see this darkness start to form around us and remember that the cycle concerns not just birth, life, and death – but the gestation, the pre-birth, conception, inception stage that is essential for healthy and true growth. It is the New Year in the sense that we are preparing to go underground, to premeditate the coming year, spend the cold dark months in thought, preparation, and planning. This is important, both to recover from the period of intense action just lived through and to build new strength and new connections for the time of action to come. Traditionally in Ireland, all social arrangements were planned in the Winter, from Samhain onwards. There were gatherings and feasts aplenty, perhaps to metaphorically stick up two fingers to the coming Winter and enjoy what they had while they had it. The past was remembered and the future planned for.

It was the time when all agricultural work had to be finished or abandoned; the herds came down from the mountains, and the men and women were reunited as a tribe to live out the Winter period together. The return of all those who had been away from the home may have been another connection to the return of those who were dead and gone, for the resting realm of the dead within the Otherworld, at this time of change, was not so far away that the honoured dead could not return home as the living did. The spirits of the land had no further compunction to cooperate with the tribe until Imbolg, at the earliest. The idea still survives that the blackberries here aren't safe to be eaten after Hallowe'en. We were told as kids that the Púca spits on them and makes them poisonous after that. Samhain was always a time for inward turning, for the Otherworld to come to more prominence than it had been in the bright heat and light of the Summer's sun. Many tales include weirdness issuing from the Otherworld, as well as easier access to the other realms, as the changeover causes the worlds to interlay.

Samhain, or Hallowe'en, is the main 'time between times', when the barriers between the worlds is at its thinnest and we can most easily see or feel across the bridges. In practical terms and non-flowery language, this means that it is especially a time for divination, magical activity and communing with spirits, both those of our ancestors, and those passing who may or may not wish us well – and, sometimes, those who need our help. We have lived the year and experienced the turning to its fullest, and now is the time to reflect on the accumulated wisdom and prepare for the long months ahead. The Goddess may meet the God in his Otherworld dwelling, or perhaps they may meet by a river in this world... for this is the time to clear the path for what may lie ahead.

For us to celebrate this festival in a modern context, there are some essential elements our celebration should contain.

Respect for the Dead

This can be in the form of a Dumb Supper, as outlined in the previous section, or perhaps with a platter of food/drink laid outside when the household retires for the night. During any actual ritual that is performed, there should be a quiet time taken, a space for reflection on those who have passed, both in our own lives and any who linger near the physical place of the working. A gentle and respectful reminder that the doors are open this night, that they may be free to move on, can be helpful. This is also an appropriate time for any who are capable enough to engage in spiritualism activity or specific contact with the dead.

Sacrifice

Most of us won't have any stock that needs culling. In lieu of looking at our neighbour's sheep, or their cats and dogs, with new interest, it might be better to symbolically sacrifice for Samhain. This doesn't have to involve bleeding oneself for the land, though I will point out that our own blood is very powerful. Menstrual blood, for example, is a natural shedding and expulsion of life-nurturing materials, usually accompanied by pain or at least physical discomfort. It makes a good sacrificial offering, but of course not everyone menstruates. We do, however, all carry blood in our veins. Shedding a drop or two can be a powerful act, but it is not necessary by any means. Personally, I do always give **something** of myself in honour of the harvest and the land during this ritual. It can be a lock of hair, nail clippings, or body fluids. It can be as simple as a spit on the ground or the fire. Anything that is of you will do. If I wish to make a specific connection to the land, I bury it. Most often it goes on the fire, as this is an element of the next part of the process.

Cleansing

The most obvious way for this to be a significant part of the festival is by lighting a bonfire. All household fires should have been extinguished from that morning; the hearth should lie cold and bare until it is re-lit from the Samhain fires, wherever possible. This is to remind us of the harsh coldness of death, before the rebirth of the new fires. If it is not practical to light your own outdoor bonfire, or there is no hearth fire in your home, at the very least a small cauldron or pot fire can be used during your working. Even a tealight or votive candle! Live flame is an incredibly important and significant part of Irish life and culture. The cauldron is appropriate as it is seen as the vessel of transformation. Raw foodstuff goes in, and sustaining meals come out. It is the womb of the Goddess, as anything can go in and be transformed. It is the Dagda's cauldron of plenty, that never runs dry. In the fires, we should ritually burn all from the old year that we wish to leave behind. This could be by writing those things on paper and burning it, or by burning objects that symbolise the things we wish to leave behind as we move into the new year. This is our cleansing, and the sacrificial offering we make of ourselves fuels this fire and is our part in the give and take of the cycle. It is often difficult to bring on the changes that we know are necessary. But this is the time to put away the things that are of no further use to us. Clear the way for new projects, new hopes, new plans.

Planning/Preparation

In your cleansing process, you will have figured out what is unnecessary to carry forward, what needed rid of. The next step is to figure out what is useful, what needs to be worked on in the coming New Year. Plans are made for carrying this through. How best to make use of your coming Winter down time - and how to ensure that you have sufficient downtime for necessary interior (both indoors and in yourself) activities. When the weather changes again and Spring has sprung, you can then step out again, sure that you are prepared and ready.

Celebration

It is a time for coming together, when tribes would reunite for Winter-based activity; the start of a new cycle. Darkness is fast approaching, but there is still time and space to celebrate light and warmth and pleasure. There should be feasting, which has always seemed to be a particularly effective way of thumbing our noses at the coming harshness of Winter. Get the fresh meats, available milk, and newly harvested fruit and vegetables while they are all still so succulent and desirable. For us, although we can technically still get all of those things all through the year, for the time being, seasonal and local foods should be used as much as possible in keeping with the cycle (and the growing environmental impact). It should also be observed, as much as possible, that outdoors work finishes at this point. Before Samhain, make sure all your outside tasks are locked down for the Winter, whether it be putting away your gardening tools or getting the last fruits collected in. Púca spit probably doesn't taste most pleasant; it's best to avoid it if possible. And once you are safely indoors, a cheery fire, a good feast, and seeing your family and friends for perhaps the first time in months will always be cause for celebration, so our ancestors wouldn't have forgotten the mead, ale, and wine.

Divination

Before the mead, ale, and wine consumption reaches its pinnacle, it is worth remembering that this is the time when the boundaries between this world and *An Saol Eile* are at the thinnest point. It is a time of trickery, of fun and games, of cross-dressing in many of the myths. Normally strict lines are blurred and everything gets a little out of focus. Usual laws, codes of behaviour, and restrictions were always more relaxed around Samhain time. In our rituals, elements of this may be brought in with games and party tricks. Typical Hallowe'en fun is always good. A lot of the games we still play have the divinatory aspects, and many of us engage in acts of focused divination at this time. The end of a ritual is the perfect time for such a thing. You are relaxed, your hunger and thirst are satiated, the work is done, and you are free to just let yourself drift into that gap between the worlds where divination lives.

As anybody who has begun to try and learn to divine the future, or see visions, will know all too well, forcing the issue will inevitably result in frustration and failure. Staring into the flames is an excellent choice of method; this is called fire scrying or pyromancy. Liquid scrying or hydromancy – looking into a liquid-filled vessel with a dark interior (a chalice of red wine, a bowl of ink, and a cauldron of water are all good choices) – is also a good option. Losing yourself in the mysterious depths can bring on excellent visionary experiences. More structured methods such as tarot card readings can also be effective, but I am all for letting it flow loosely and seeing what comes up. If you wish to use your usual tarot cards, rune stones, or ogham staves, perhaps approaching them in different ways would be a good idea. Maybe try the random pulling of cards, or throwing of runes, or meditating on the ogham letters (just focusing on them and seeing what pops into your mind, or floats through it), with no particular forced or usual structure on your divination. This is tremendously powerful when the mists of Samhain descend.

Imbolg (February 1st)

This is the first festival of Spring, the time to emerge from the darkness and begin the work outdoors, as the first births would be happening in the shape of lambs and kids. For our ancestors, this was a crucial and enjoyable time, after a Winter of very little in the way of fresh milk or foodstuffs. The first sheep's milk was considered a great delicacy. It also has a higher fat content than cow's milk so it would be just the thing to perk you up after a harsh Winter. Indeed, one of the names for this festival has been Oimelc, which may have come from 'ewe's milk', though this has been contested. This time is also known as Imbolc, a word that may be traced back to the tradition of washing at this time, from the verb *folc* (to wash or bathe) – a personal Spring cleaning, perhaps. It may come from similar to the modern Irish *imfholc*, which would mean sort of a 'great washing' or a big cleanse. A passage from Hibernica Minora, quoted in Nerys Patterson's excellent book 'Cattle Lords and Clansmen' goes thus:

> *"Tasting of each food in accordance to order, this is what is proper
>   at Imbolc: washing the hands, the feet, the head...".*

This isn't enough really on which to assume that the whole festival was based around the washing. Anybody who has spent the Winter in a grotty hut will be quite keen to wash their head, hands, and feet before a meal once Spring arrives, I would have thought. Imbolc is slightly different from the Irish term I know and use.

I personally call this festival Imbolg (pron. Ih Mullgh), which is from the modern Irish for 'in the belly'. It may also have associations with the Old Irish word *blicht* - a term for 'in milk' might be *i mblicht* - which according to the eDIL means:

1 blicht: milk , a milking, yield of milk; Transfd. of abundant yield, produce
  2 blicht: Milch, in milk, milk-giving; flowing, abundant

To me, using this name recognises the time as concerned with the firstborn of the sheep and goats, for what is in the belly will bring forth the mother's milk – but also of importance is the human birth cycle. Those of us who conceived at the Bealtaine celebration - when couples traditionally head off to the woods for the 'Greenwood Marriage' (more on this later) - would have given birth around Imbolg after a long heavy Winter of sitting around, carrying the new life within a massive belly, doing very little else. With folks being separated for their agricultural chores on May 1st, Imbolg would have been a common time for babies to be born, so for a lot of mothers who were trying to breastfeed new babies it was an especially precarious time, during which they particularly needed the nourishment of the first sheep's milk, which starts to flow about a month before the first lambs are born. So the cycle of human and animal birth and milk production are themes of paramount importance at Imbolg.

Once the tide of Winter was turned, the babes were being born, the sheep had their lambs and the milk was flowing again, thoughts would turn to cleansing out the stale and decaying air, opening up all the stores, and taking stock of what had survived and of what was in dire need of replenishment. In Irish folk tradition, this was a major happening on February 1st.

To echo the mention of the importance of washing and clearing, we see more cleansing being done traditionally, with the fires at this time. An interesting addition we came to naturally in our own working group was the sweeping away of the old at Imbolg. This is, of course, quite a big theme since Samhain; all through the dark cold months the old and worn out will have been worked on and gotten rid of from our lives. The last cobwebs and

116

remnants of the old year and the harshness of the Winter are supposed to be finally and thoroughly swept away in preparation for the new growth and fresh hope to follow. It is on a physical, outward level rather than the inward cleansing and preparation of the Winter.

When we first came to the house I lived in when I wrote this book, and a small few folk started to try and work together as a group there, we were terribly unprepared. At Imbolg, we had no broom – nothing to sweep away the last cobwebs and remnant of the Old Year with. We only realised this just before we all braved the grove to start the outside part of the ritual. Luckily, I have a thing for Winter holiday decorations. (Bear with me. This is going somewhere relevant, I promise.) I love the sparkles, the pretty lights, and reflections. Our tree from the Winter Solstice had been massive, and I was loathe to get rid of our first (pretty lights) tree in our new home. So, we simply took the monster evergreen down and chopped the top 3 feet off. It was then nailed to a board, stuck atop the stove in the parlour (taking up A LOT less room than its parent), and redecorated. I got to keep my pretty lights, and the family also had the use of the room again without an intake of breath and pine needles to pass by the monster.

Even at Imbolg, the start of February – yes, two months after Midwinter – the tree top with its sparkles had only just come down. I tended to get until the end of January out of a tree if I kicked the Taurean stubbornness into gear and stared down all opposition. So, as we stood at the back door on a freezing Imbolg night, wondering what we were to do for a besom broom at this late hour, my eyes settled on the treetop, with its still bushy branches (but dried-out needles). Pure natural wood, a firm representation of the Old Year, and totally expendable into the bargain. We could use it to not just sweep away, but to represent and collect the Old energies, and then burn it when we were done. Spring cleaning in its truest form! Of course, this meant the fire had to be lit outside, and stay lit, but that was okay. Sort of.

You see, the **original** ritual plan had been only to get some sort of natural fire in the circle, even if it had to be a lantern. It was pouring rain at that stage, and there was not much dry fuel lurking about the place. As you can probably imagine, my **new and improved** ritual plan went down like a lead balloon. But I convinced most of them it was a great idea, and, amid some muttering and grumbling as the wet wood hissed and spit and refused to take, the fire was eventually lit and circle began. The holiday tree broom worked astoundingly well, with all of us able to firmly pour our worn-out remnants into its branches during the *tuathal* (pron. Too-ah-all, meaning 'against the sun, to the left' and used to banish) round of the circle. It blazed appropriately and burned to nothing in the cleansing light of the Imbolg fire. This became a coven tradition from then on. Seeing the Old Year blaze to fiery demise on the cleansing and strengthening Imbolg fire is a sight and a feeling I still won't deprive myself of by choice. It is an amazing end to the remnants of the year and a fitting cremation to the parts we work so hard to change and improve on and leave behind, from Samhain to Imbolg, to prepare for fresh, strong growth.

Imbolg is the festival of the Tuatha Dé Danann Goddess Brighid. When looking at her, we saw that she had three main roles: inspirer of poets, patroness of smiths, and keeper of the home and health. In all of these roles, fire is of great importance - the fire of inspiration and creativity, the fire of the forge, and the fire of healing and the hearth. In the modern interpretation of *Lá Fhéile Bhride* (pron. Law Ail-ah Vreedj-eh), which is Bridget's Feast Day, we can still see the upholding of such fire-based traditions. In her monastery in County Kildare, a perpetual fire was kept burning in her honour, tended by 20 nuns, with no men being granted access to the enclosure or sight of the fire. This is a remnant of older traditions of priestesses tending the Goddess's sacred fire - and of it being a particularly female mystery. The festival we celebrate is concerned very much with the role of women, women's functions, and women's mysteries (this is relevant for, and welcoming to, anyone who identifies as a woman, in case that needs to be made clear). It is also a celebration of light, for although the first of February can still be quite dark, cold, and even snowy, there is an inkling of the returning light of Spring, with the defiant light being lit and kept burning through the changing darkness. Lighting the fire and rejoicing in it at this time is a sign of encouragement for the return of the sun's power.

A good representation of these things still used in Ireland is the St.

Brighid's cross I mentioned previously. It is a solar cross, called a *crosóg* (pron. Cruss-oh-g), which means 'little cross', or a *Cros Bhríde* (pron. Cruss Vreedj-eh), which is 'Brighid's Cross'. It is made from pretty much anything, but most usually woven or plaited rushes or straw. We have a lot of rushes and straw here. The *crosóg* represents the continuing cycle of the sun, the year, and the seasons, as they turn and turn about. The unending *deiseal* (pron. jesh-ill, meaning 'sunwise, to the right') rotation of the cross's power represents the increasing collection of abundance and the sun's life-giving energy. We most commonly see the familiar Ulster form of this cross, with four arms; but they come in all shapes and sizes, and many areas and even families have their own designs carried through for generations.

This is the time at which the women go and lay Biddy's bed. This uses a Biddy doll, or *Brideóg* (pron. Breedj-oh-g), made up of grasses and whatever herbs or growth is available, laid into a made-up 'bed' on the hearth of your home or the group's working space. If there is a person in the group or partaking in the Imbolg ritual who wishes to get pregnant that coming year, they should be the one who makes the Biddy, binding into it their hopes and dreams of fertility and plenty to come. This is not to say (I hasten to add for those who have performed the task of creating a Biddy doll unwittingly!) that everybody who makes such an item will fall pregnant. It is simply an appropriate carrier for that type of hopes and desires, as it is for the more exoteric or practical aspects of one's life. Fertility for the coming year does not have to mean a physical pregnancy, after all. Inviting the blessing of Brighid, in the person of the Brideóg doll, to your home and your hearth will keep the fires of inspiration, the healing and transformative fires of her magical power, burning brightly in the times ahead. By binding one's wishes into the doll as it is made, you effectively name it for the person, the coven, or the land – whatever you feel the designation of her aid should be. In our group it was always the women who laid the bed and who called her in while in a huddle around the bed; while the men stood back and pretended to look busy.

For us to celebrate this festival in a modern context, there are some essential elements our celebration should contain.

Cleansing

During the day of the festival, there should be a good clear out of the house – a Spring cleaning, if you will. Open all cupboards. Decide what needs to stay, what needs to go, and what you need to stock up on and replenish. It is also a good time to re-examine your Samhain records (it is essential to keep accurate records and diaries of every magical working you do, at the very least, and at best a daily record is an excellent way of charting your own progress and learning from your mistakes and successes), and take a stock of everything.

Have you accomplished what you set out to do over the Winter? Are you ready for the coming Spring? What can you check off your To Do list, as done? What do you need to put more energy into? What is not relevant anymore and can be disregarded or put aside, for this year at least? This is not to be used as an excuse to beat yourself up for not doing enough; it is simply an honest appraisal of your progress. When the evening time comes, particular attention should be paid to each participant's personal ablutions before any ritual. Most of us won't enter into a magical working while sweaty and smelly, but the pre-ritual wash isn't always given the due care and attention it deserves - from a ritualistic point of view. In our case, it was too often a rushed shower while stressing over how late we were in starting. It is, however, the appropriate time for the shedding of your everyday cares before you enter your sacred space, for any working should not really be scrimped on or rushed. At Imbolg, it is particularly essential. A large bowl should be placed at the entrance point of your circle or working space, filled with fresh spring water and appropriate herbs, flowers, or oils. Everybody who enters the space can first wash their hands, feet, and head in this specially prepared spring water.

Sustenance and Birth

Milk should be given to each participant as they enter the space; if you work alone, immediately drink milk from a cup or chalice. If you can get fresh sheep's milk, wonderful, and my, you are a dedicated soul! Goat's milk will do as an excellent second choice. Indeed, if you could be involved in milking the goat that morning, it would be a wonderful preparation... I did get to the point in my ritual work, at one stage, where this was happening. Of course, ordinary cow's milk (or even a plant based milk, in a pinch!) will do just fine if you don't have access to sheep or goats. Partaking in the symbolic first milk of Imbolg represents not just fresh sustenance after the Winter period, but also serves as a reminder of the flow of our own fertility and the importance of birthing and new life being sustained and nurtured at this time. A symbolic birth of any new ideas or projects can be brought in here.

Lighting of Fires

As at Samhain, you can light your own outdoor bonfire, a hearth fire in your home, or a small cauldron fire to be used during your working. A cleansing sweep of your space can be done, using the old Midwinter festival tree if possible, or a bundle of branches taken from it. If you have a bonfire, you chuck the whole lot on and watch that baby burn away the Old Year. If your home fires are more sedate, the bundle of branches used for sweeping or even a twig or small branch of the tree itself can be used. If you don't burn your tree at this time, make sure it is taken off your premises, away from your home, by the next morning at the very latest. Last year's *crosóga* (crosses) should also be burned at this stage in the proceedings. There's no point in letting the Old Year hang around once you say goodbye to it.

Brideóg and Crosóga

The Biddy's bed should be laid by the women, with a pre-prepared Brideóg doll placed in it. An invocation to (inviting her into yourself), or evocation of (inviting her to your working space, but outside of you) Brighid can be done at this stage. She should be invited to your home in whatever way you choose. As we have seen, I am a firm believer in addressing your Gods in their native tongue so something similar to the following can be used:

> *'Tar isteach, tar isteach! Ligigí Bríd isteach! Tá céad míle fáilte romhat, a bhean uasail!'*
> *(pron. 'Tar iss-chyok tar iss-chyok, Lih-gi-gee Breedj iss-chyok, Taw kayd meal-ah fawl-cha roe-ath, ah van oo-assall!').*

It means, 'Come in, come in! Let Brighid inside! A hundred thousand welcomes to you, noble woman!'

Specific reference should be made to her triplicate form (perhaps with three women playing the parts of Brighid and her aspects/sisters) and also to the triple fires (the fire of inspiration and creativity, the fire of the forge, and the fire of healing and the hearth). Please note - this is NOT a Maiden, Mother, and Crone thing, at all - that is not part of the native Irish tradition. If Brigid's crosses have been made, there should be one for each participant. They should be blessed at this stage, and the wishes and hopes for health, wealth, and abundance be willed into them. Afterwards, everyone can hang their *crosóg* over their own hearth, or in a central location in their home, until next year. (We have a class on Brighid over at the Irish Pagan School, given by one of our native teachers, so make sure you're on the mailing list there!)

Bealtaine (April 30th)

This is the other half of the year, turning again toward Samhain. It also is a time of great change, as the major transition from Winter to Summer occurs. *Bealtaine* (pron. Bee-Yowl-tinneh in my standardised Irish, and Bal-tin-eh in some other dialect voices) is still the name in modern Irish for the month of May. I used to think this meant, 'Bel's fire', based on the available research at the original time of writing. The prevailing current scholarly opinion on that is probably best summed up in the following succinct quote from the Online Etymology Dictionary:

> *"The rubbish about Baal, Bel, Belus imported into the word from the Old Testament and classical antiquity, is outside the scope of scientific etymology. [OED]"*

According to the etymologists there, the correct meaning is:

> *"probably literally 'blazing fire', from PIE root ***bhel**- (1) 'to shine, flash, burn' + Old Irish ten 'fire', from PIE *tepnos, related to Latin tepidus 'warm', from PIE root *tep- 'to be hot'.*

Still completely correct though, is the fact that *Bealtaine* is the only proper name for the festival in this country, where we have a living linguistic term for it. So when working in an Irish tradition, versions such as Beltane and Beltaine should be used with caution. Or just not at all.

A note for the second edition, based on actual social media conversations I've had to have... Beltane is not the English version of the Irish word *Bealtaine*. Beltane is the dumbed down anglicized 'simplified' version of it because 'Irish has too many vowels/is too difficult/is unnecessary', and when you use Beltane in an Irish (or Celtic, as other cultures have their own spellings - choose one!) Pagan context you are contributing to colonial erasure, at best. Once again, please don't do that.

This was the time to remove the cattle and sheep from the temptation of neighbours' cornfields and up the hills for grazing, so big movements occurred in the tribes. Come Spring and Summer, it is a sheep's natural inclination to move uphill, so it was easier to just follow them on their natural routes rather than try and restrain them. Though some would remain to tend the homes and take care of the sick or elderly, most women and children would leave to live at the Summer pastures after Bealtaine for the upland grazing, and would not return until Samhain time. This is called Booleying in later times, as it carried on through the centuries, into living memory. The men would stay behind, some to tend the crops and homesteads, but most to prepare for warfare, in ancient times. There was every chance that those who were about to split apart might not see each other again, and, even if they did, it would be in half a year's time, with perhaps a brief reprieve at Lúnasa for some, with all hands on deck for the harvest. I would imagine it made for some fun and games at Bealtaine time, with the last party, as the people let their hair down and made sure they had lots to remember each other by.

With such shifts in population, it was a time when accounts were settled, taxes and tithes called in, obligations met, and payments made. This can translate into our own cycle, too, in the way of assessing what is owed to you, what you owe to yourself and to others and settling your accounts. When we are coming to the Summer in true, anything we have promised ourselves that we needed to do or have done needs to be taken care of now, if it has not been seen to before. It is a continuation of the cyclical appraisal process begun at Samhain and carried on at Imbolg.

The magic of Bealtaine is concerned with protecting your interests, historically ensuring that the first fruits and first crops went to their rightful owners and that all was fertile enough to provide what was necessary. There has been archaeological evidence found at the summit of the Hill of Uisneach – which is a central point of this island and (as a traditional Druidic stronghold) an incredibly important spiritual site – of massive scorching on the earth, containing the charred remains of many animals. Dr. Roseanne Schot has done some amazing work there in recent years. This evidence ties right in with folklore reports of ritual bonfires lit in the presence of a massive gathering of people. Sacrifices were said to have been made in the sacred fires on behalf of those present. There are also reports of druids and others, in various parts of Ireland, lighting two tremendous bonfires side by side, 'with great incantations', and driving cattle and other livestock between them. This was a measure against diseases and sickness that might otherwise afflict the livestock. The fire acted as a cleansing, purification, and a protective force. The livestock was driven close enough between the fires to be scorched by them. Is this a remnant of the sacrifices? Not giving the animals to the fires, but at least giving a taste of them, in the form of their hair. At the very least, the smoke and heat could have the effect of clearing some external parasites and even mild infections, as well as spiritual cleansing potential with smoke purification methods which can also be seen in many other cultures.

The protective magic was carried on in a lot of ways. As this is another time of great change, the boundaries again are thin; though it perhaps does not seem quite so scary with Summer coming on instead of Winter. Nevertheless, it is still a time when harmful or malevolent magic held great power. Those who were looking to protect their own interests could often most easily do it by damaging yours. We see a lot of significance placed with the Rowan tree - known as *Caorthann* (Sorbus aucuparia) - which was a great charm against Witches (those who carried out destructive magic, in the given interpretation of the time). Rowan (known elsewhere as Mountain Ash) branches and twigs were tied into a cross shape with red string and placed at doors and windows, or tied into the tails of your animals, to protect your interests. This would dispel the power of unfriendly Otherworld or malevolent energies directed at you and yours.

The trickery and cross-gender confusion we saw at Samhain was very much in evidence here, too. Many supposedly female roles in parades and plays were played by young men. This may be a reminder of the changing of the time and strength of the Winter hag to the Summer energy of the bright young male. The (often older) female form would then be shed and the fresh young male could emerge from that shell to continue on as normal with the year. On the lines of dressing up, the Fool archetype held a strong place in many festivals and rituals at this time of year. As the Fool or jester lived his or her life outside normal boundaries and strictures at all times, it was thought that such a figure could aid the necessary transition. Before the sanitisation of these festivities, there may have been blatant exaggerations of sexual exploits included in the general mayhem of parades, fairs, and gatherings at which a lot of folk were dressed up and outside the bounds of their normal behaviour, with the added freedom of not having to see the other gathering attendees for a good while afterwards. So, sort of like an office party, without the embarrassing aftermath of actually having to work with those people day in, day out.

The obvious sexual fertility theme we see at Bealtaine had stronger implications: it was the necessary breaking of the infertile Winter's grip on the land. Physical and sexual interaction taking place actually on the land was hugely important to wake it up after the sterility of Winter. So the 'Greenwood Marriage', as it is known in modern Pagan terms, was a common occurrence at this festival. Couples would stroll off into the wood and the fields to, ahem... interact. Perhaps a more official, ritualised Sacred Marriage between King and the Land took place as a matter of course at Bealtaine, but the people's couplings represented as well the ritual significance of the myth in which the God force comes of age and weds the Sovereign Goddess or Lady of the Land.

The sun's power is a tremendously important theme at Bealtaine. We have seen it in celebrations of sexuality and waking up the land, for it is the sun's rays that actually perform this inspiring duty. The increasing warmth, light, and penetrating rays shake the earth from the last hold of the Winter period. Though the God force represents the sun in its coming maturity and power, there are many traditions of making sure to actually view the rising of the sun, usually from your local sacred hilltop. This took place at dawn on May Day, which is why Bealtaine Eve is the logical time for ritual. You can either stay up in an all-night vigil (or revel) and greet the sun on May Day morn, or you can rise from your own bed to welcome its rays. This is the strengthening and healing fire we see through the rituals, but there is also the presence of many fire and water traditions. Dew drops gathered on May

Day morning, which had collected the fire of the rising sun, are bottled and kept for healing and beautification purposes throughout the year. Any pool or body of water that captures the dawn rays is seen as powerfully beneficial, for any of us who are hardy enough to take a dip in them.

I would also like to point out that the maypole so long associated with this festival, though great fun on the day, is not an Irish or even a Celtic custom. It's English. Some Celtic communities have borrowed from it over the years, using living trees in some cases but, as we are sticking to what is truly ours here, we'll leave that particular piece of misinformation to one side.

Ireland does have its own May Bush traditions though. I have seen this as a hawthorn bush, as a holly bush decorated with hawthorn twigs and leaves, or sometimes as a bunch of hawthorn branches tied together into a bush shape. It is decorated with bright things - coloured ribbons, eggshells, and all sorts of trappings - and given centre stage in the proceedings. Sometimes it is a bush at the front of a property, that is set on fire and the smoke wafted over house and/or land, for purification and protective purposes.

For us to celebrate this festival in a modern context, there are some essential elements our celebration should contain.

Allocation of Resources

Before moving into the Summertime in true, we need to make sure we can leave only clear air behind us. It is a good idea to try to allocate and structure your time now; it is too easy to get caught up in Summer play these days. But if we take the *Tuatha*, or tribe, as a model – each person's talent was put to work where it would have maximum effect and usefulness. All bases are covered. Do the same within your own family or even your own life: put your talents to work to take maximum advantage of the coming time. There is hard physical work ahead, with lots of attention to the practical aspects of our existence, whether you are watering potted plants a trillion times a day (those 'water-retaining' composts just don't work well enough if the sun is shining hard!) or ensuring your field crop is growing well, tending flocks, or bringing the kids to the park and swimming every time they ask, you will want to be able to put yourself 100 percent into those physical tasks, and it is good to step into that phase with a clear head. You will sleep better, too. In our world, we should look to pay off niggling debts, clear up misunderstandings, clarify relationships, collect what is owed to us, and generally settle our accounts both ways. Another examination of your Samhain plans is also necessary here, and settlement made on any outstanding issues you haven't addressed thus far from that. Keep a record of all of this!

Lightning of Fires

This was primarily the job of the men in many places, and the fires were cleansing, sacrificial and protective. If possible, light two bonfires outdoors, close together but with enough space to pass through. Put actual bones in them, and make sure to keep the ashes to spread on your fields/garden/houseplants. If bonfires are not practical - yes, I do know that not everyone lives in rural areas and can do such things without a risk of starting forest or bush fires... please take care! - try two lanterns or even two candles side by side. It's not quite the same, but we do what needs must. As at Samhain, anything you wish to rid yourself of, primarily health problems and those concerned with the physical, can be thrown on the fire as you pass between. A symbolic representation of this will do, or the sickness/problem written on some paper. It is unnecessary (and probably illegal) to chuck your ailing mother-in-law into the bonfire. You don't have to get yourself burned on the way through either, and do be quite careful of this. The Bealtaine fires often get hungry and claim their own sacrifice. Many a cloak or trailing sleeve has died a death in such a fashion and, for those of us with long flowing locks, extra care is recommended. Any protection magic that you feel the need for should be done now. Your hearth and home can be safeguarded and protected; look to taking care of your own. Traditionally, this has been a perfect time for malevolent workings to the detriment of others, if it means the increase of your own holdings - not that I am recommending such a practice, of course, but if you were that way inclined, this is when to do it. This is also why I recommend that you look to protecting your own home and holdings at Bealtaine, just in case. There is no harm in being prepared.

Boundary Crossover

This is the start of the fun and games. Create and dress your May Bush. Nominate one person to play *An Amadán Mór* (pron. On Omma-dawn More), 'the Great Fool' of the proceedings, and direct the fun and games. Dress up. Sing songs. Play games. Ask riddles. Tell jokes. Laugh and cavort and caper to your heart's content. Eat, drink, and be merry. This obviously works to full advantage if there is a large crowd or group, but if you are working and celebrating alone, it can also be a time to test your own boundaries. Indulge in something you haven't been brave enough to try before. Find out what you enjoy doing and what you don't, at a time between times when all rules are suspended. Aid the changing year on year by changing yourself, and your surroundings, in a way that is appropriate to you and your life. Even if it only lasts the evening, splash out, experiment, and enjoy.

Fertility

Sexual or fertility magic is particularly potent now. Feel free, literally, to explore your wants and desires, in a mutually consensual and safe manner, of course. Offer your efforts (and any leftover fluids or elixir, but only if you are experienced in that sort of magic and know the risks/responsibilities that come with it) to the land spirits or even the Sidhe to stir them up again and - maybe - to get them on your side for the rest of the year. Historically, for those who hadn't conceived a child thus far in the year, this may have been the last chance, and so it was tackled with renewed vigour on this final night together. So whether your wish for fertility concerns actual babies, or material bounty, a concentrated blast of energy in that direction on Bealtaine Eve is a pretty sure-fire way to bring about the conception of your wishes.

Acknowledgment of the Sun's Energy

Get out of your bed and go watch the sunrise. Or stay up all night, climb a hill, and greet its fertilising rays at dawn. Collect the dew drops as they are touched by the golden light. Alternatively, find a pool or lake in which to bathe, to absorb the fire-in-water magic of the morning. Catch a sample of the water where the Bealtaine sun sparkles on its surface to use through the year for its particular healing and restorative properties.

Lúnasa (August 1st)

Lúnasa (pron. Loo-Na-Sah) is the climax of the four main Irish festivals: the harvest of the fruits of all previous labours. Some of the earliest crops in Ireland - oats, wheat and barley - could have been harvested at the beginning of August. Reaping the first fruits of the harvest is a vastly important theme at Lúnasa, as it would have been eagerly awaited. July was known in Ireland as *Iúil an Ghorta* (pron. Ee-ool on Gur-tha), 'July of the Famine', or *Iúil an Chabáiste* (pron. Ee-ool on Kob-aw-shtha), 'July of the Cabbages'. Farmers were down to their last oats and turf, and potatoes in later years (when we had potatoes). As a general point of interest, it may be worth bearing in mind the origins of the so-called 'Irish Potato'. One story holds that Sir John Hawkins introduced the potato into Ireland in 1565, and another says Sir Walter Raleigh first grew it here in 1585. Either way, though conditions in Ireland were (and still are) generally ideal for its prolific cultivation; it is certainly not a native Irish plant, nor was it grown here in 'ancient' times.

So, after a long lean month or two working through the last of the previous year's stores, when the crops of the time were finally ready to harvest, there probably would have been much in the way of celebration. Ripening wild berries, tender young vegetables, fresh sweet nuts, mature greens: I can only imagine just how important they would have been to those who had just spent July surviving on old oats and cabbages.

As we have already discussed, the Tailteann fair (located at what is now

130

Teltown, in County Meath) that came to be associated with the Lúnasa festival was centered around honouring Tailtiu, the Goddess who fostered Lugh after Manannán Mac Lir had taken him in. As a Goddess of the land, the harvest theme would have made her an appropriate patroness, saying thanks for abundance and plenty. She was buried under a large mound and so, in her honour, the fairs and games were held at a height. This still survives in some places, where locals gather on the summits of local hills, for their Garland Sunday or Bilberry Sunday festivities a little before Lúnasa 'officially' begins (this was the last Sunday of July, most often) - when they reap the benefits of any local fruit, flowers, and nuts in their own mini-harvest. There would be faction fighting between the young men from neighbouring areas, and horse racing aplenty if the site was anywhere near flat ground. Many of the sites for the festivals were at some distance from the living enclosures and villages of those who celebrated. With such a strenuous trek to attend these events, there may have been an element of pilgrimage for those who could make the journey and so were able to attend and participate. We see this still carried through in the pilgrimage to Croagh Patrick (the sacred peak of Connacht) to this day, as part of our living tradition and heritage.

As Brighid presided at Imbolg, now we see Lugh in prominence – with corresponding associations of traditional women's activities then, and traditional men's activities now. Of course, those restrictive gender roles are not applicable today, but an acknowledgement of how it used to be is appropriate. The ewes were removed from their parental responsibilities at this time, sheared and washed so the smells of the mother were eliminated from the lamb, and thus the bond between mother and child was broken. The weaning happened abruptly, and this brought the ewes back to a production and fertility cycle quite quickly, so we see a movement from the role of nurturing mother to that of sexual activity and conception once again. Although the sexual lives of sheep don't hold much relevance to most of us today, the theme of such movement is an important one, as it holds with the charge of more male-focused energy that comes to the fore at Lúnasa. There are many Victorian missives on the scandalous behavior of boys and girls at this time. There were suggestive activities concerning flower garlands, dancing, and singing, as well as naked horse-back riding... but, as to how openly sexual it all got, we are not too sure. After all, it wouldn't have been too difficult to scandalise your average Victorian.

The importance and celebration of the male virility and vital sexual and fertilising energy can be seen in its modern form at the Puck Fair in Kerry. This event is still held in early August, in a town called Killorglin. A male, or 'Puck', goat is crowned as King of the Fair, and a coronation ceremony and parade are held in his honour on the first day. He is then raised up over the proceedings on a tower and treated with many accolades during the three-day fair. A lot of folks still believe the Puck goat of honour to be strongly symbolic of sexuality and fertility.

Fire and water is a continuing theme, but as the sun has turned from an encouraging light and warmth-bringing entity, to the searing and crop-scorching possible enemy, water takes prominence here. Lugh shows his full power by bringing stability to the sun's searing heat when he kills his grandfather Balor, whose blazing eye represents, as we have seen, the sun's more destructive energy. Traditions hold with a dampening of the Summer's power, as all flowers (Summer blooms) that are harvested, used, or carried on this day are to be buried under the earth once the day is done. Where cattle were driven through fires for protection at Bealtaine, horses are driven through water for purification at Lúnasa. Horse racing is a prominent activity, as at a fair the mares would be run in competitions to show their speed and agility, and thus were their foals valued by the onlookers.

Alexei Kondratiev put forth the idea of a reunion of opposites being brought into effect here. Cattle represent the land energies, with cows as the nurturing aspect and bulls as the destructive, and horses were symbolic of the Tribe in its sovereignty of the land. Cows were connected to water – Bóann the cow/river Goddess being a prime example of this – and horses connected with solar energies in the way of its fire force and drive. As mentioned, when the cattle were healed and protected by being driven through the fires at Bealtaine, so the horses were purified by being raced and forced to swim through rivers, lakes, or the sea - thus bringing about the reunion of opposite force and achieving an essential balance.

Horse fairs still survive and thrive at Lúnasa, one of the most famous being the aforementioned Puck Fair in Kerry. The tradition of the fair itself was an important one for drawing together the isolated people of any community. The word for a fair in modern Irish is *aonach* (pron. A [like the a in ABC) Nock), which seems to have stemmed from the root of *aon*, which means 'one'. As we have such terms as *aontaigh* (pron. A ontee), 'to unite', and *aontas* (pron. A ontass), 'union', it follows that *aontach* may have originally meant a reunion or a gathering. Indeed the plural of *aonach* is *aontaí*, which now means 'fairs', but is pronounced the same as *aontaigh*, 'to unite', High kings, kings, and tribal chieftains all held *aontaí* of various sizes at Lúnasa. The emphasis is very much on community spirit, social connection, and celebration. Indeed, the Puck Fair Website directly states:

It is a time when old friends meet, when new friendships are forged,
   And the cares of everyday living are put on hold.

With the gathering of a populace who rarely got to interact, there were many games of skill and strength at the *aontaí,* and poets and bards got to show their stuff, too, with recitations and song demonstrating their craft and all adding to the convivial atmosphere. The games were also an expression of the masculine energy expressing itself once more – a flexing of the muscles if you will. Lúnasa was the time for temporary marriages and seasonal hiring to take place; when people looked for their Winter lodgings and earned their keep all through, being released and paid 'per month spent' in the arrangement, come the following Bealtaine. Perhaps the games and displays of skill and talent were to show the males off to their full capacity, so, as with the horse racing, people were in competition to show their speed and agility, and thus were they valued by the on-lookers. Not quite the year and a day temporary handfasting we see in Neo-Paganism, but a root of it perhaps.

For us to celebrate this festival in a modern context, there are some essential elements our celebration should contain.

Reaping the harvest

This should be both symbolic, and in actuality where possible. Most of what you have sown, given birth to, and nurtured – at Samhain, Imbolg, and Bealtaine – should be starting to show the benefits at this stage. You should now have some eggs in your basket, so to speak – something to enjoy, even if it's only a little satisfaction, the beginning of your comeback. Your 'crop' may not have reached full maturity yet, it may even take another cycle to do so, but content yourself with some small reward and self-congratulation for the work you have put in thus far, and give yourself a break! At Lúnasa it is all right to sit and enjoy your previous hard work, for once.

With regard to the physical harvest, whether wild or cultivated, some sort of reaping of crops should be engaged in. If you have nothing growing yourself (and it is definitely worth planting something, anything, around Imbolg so you will have something to harvest at Lúnasa) or nothing in the locality (check your nearest woods and fields for safe fruits or nuts to pick), then a trip to a fruit-picking farm or even a garden centre (to purchase something you can later reap - an exchange of value in lieu of labour, at least, is important here) should be arranged on or near Lúnasa. Those with access to nothing more than a flower pot can have something that they have grown themselves to pick as part of the ritual, even if it is only an inedible flower. This 'official picking' should be done as part of your ritual, with the harvest then used later on in the ritual.

Lúnasa Games

Physical feats and competitions of dexterity, speed, agility, and strength, as well as tests of mental dexterity, creative ability, or vocal talent, are all appropriate here. If possible, some sort of swimming or horse riding/racing event is particularly appropriate. Please be careful if fording any rivers; I have no wish to see any of you drowned in the name of authenticity. If you work alone, it may be difficult to incorporate this aspect of the festival into your celebration. Anything that represents to you an expression of the focused, active, driving force that is typically associated with 'male energy' here, will suffice. It may seem to be quite mundane, but anything done with the right intent can be magical and celebratory. Have a 'gallop' around your garden. Go for a swim. Challenge your dad to a game of chess. (The Irish equivalent was *fidhchell* [pron. Fee-kell], a board game that Lugh is said to have invented.) Trek to a local hill or summit and run around a bit on that. Gathering folks together is an aspect of this time that really should not be ignored, in the spirit of the fair. So if you normally work alone, do try and spend at least some of the Lúnasa period with like-minded people.

Expression of Sexuality

Whether alone or in a group this too should not be ignored. If you are on your own, it might be nice to dress in a way in which you feel particularly sexy or explore your own sexual needs in some way. When you are with other people, a game can be devised with couples chasing each other. What happens when you catch your intended is entirely up to you both, as long as it is between enthusiastically consenting adults! Dancing can be used to entice the intended, and would have been part of traditional Irish fair courtship. We're not necessarily talking striptease here folks, anything physical and close contact can be... enticing, between the right people! Use your imagination, and have some fun. See if you can find some Victorians to scandalise.

Portrayals of Lugh's Energy

As we welcomed Brighid to our homes at Imbolg, we should recognise Lugh himself in the Lúnasa festival. Some themes of his myths are his multiple-talents, which we have explored through the games, and the dampening of the potentially scorching Summer energy, which leads us toward the Winter period of the year. Anything that mitigates the Summer or the scorching sun will be relevant here, from a ritual reenactment of Lugh slaying Balor, to burying or 'drowning' the flowers that have been used during the celebration.

135

(We will have a whole class on Lugh over at the Irish Pagan School, given by one of our native teachers and full of fantastic resources, so make sure you check that out!)

Trading and Agreements

It would be particularly appropriate to have a barter session, trading some of your own harvest or accomplishments at this stage in the festival. If you have grown yourself some succulent early carrots, see if Jimmy will trade you some of his strawberries for them. Or if you set yourself the task of learning to knit or sculpt way back at Samhain, try and arrange for some of the products of your newfound skill to find good homes with your friends, always for good returns. Very little is gifted at an Irish fair; everything has its own price or value, though usually, the price is open to argument before the agreement. Contracts can be most successfully entered into on this day, fittingly invoking Lugh again in his role as the "God who presided over oaths and bargains". Marriages, particularly those entered into on a more temporary or mutually functional basis, are traditionally held at Lúnasa, which makes it a rather appropriate time for a handfasting.

Feasting

Enjoy the fruits of your labour (or the fruits of somebody else's labour which you have paid/exchanged them something of value for, if you are not inclined to grow your own). Celebrate your new contract, marriages, or skills. Eat, drink, and be merry - again. Exult in the Summer's pleasures, to the fullest of your ability, for next we turn to Samhain and the start of the Winter period once again.

As we begin the cycle once more at the Samhain New Year, and again work through each festival in turn, things begin to clarify a bit more. Keep your record faithfully as you turn with the seasons. You will soon begin to see how things will slot into place, as you tune in to an easier way of working your life. Experiment with each festival, challenge yourself to find ways of expressing the elements and themes outlined here, and develop your own based on further research and study of the season and traditions. This is by no means a full account of Irish life through the year. There is much for you to explore and incorporate into your own life when it is relevant and realistic. Enjoy!

Lora's Note: Besides those mentioned above for Brighid and Lugh, I have created a couple of class resources - 'Seasons and Sacred Cycles', the Fire Festivals Series, and more - that you may want to go to for a deeper dive at https://IrishPaganSch ool.com

6

Stages of a Witch's Life

One of the reasons any of us work in a group is to have other people with whom to share our life experiences. In the past, when people heard me use the word coven as a description of our working group, and especially when they knew we had worked the Wiccan ways previously, they often fear a 'form without emotion' way of working – silence, servitude, no true connection or feeling – that traditional Wicca seems to have a reputation for.

We did use what we learned through traditional Wicca in that coven, and some techniques learned from experiences with other magical groups, such as the O.T.O. Foundation, to give a structure to some of our work, especially during a person's initial training. We also, however, had seen how bad Wicca can be when it doesn't work. When the High Priestess is the sole focus and needs to be consistently in the spotlight, when the High Priest views coven meetings as a hunting ground for nubile (and often vulnerable) young women, and when the rituals are empty role-play as an excuse for the drinking session that comes after. Of course, none of those things were exclusive to the Wiccan tradition, but rather too common through NeoPaganism at a certain time period.

We decided to keep only what we knew to be effective, and working: formal ritual only to serve a specific purpose, as a part and not the whole of our magic. Our coven was a bit of a mishmash of 'let's try this and see what happens'. We were breaking new ground, though trying to figure out what from the old ground was still useful. The more formal magic was useful for training, and we also used it in the initiations and some of our spell-working or divination-focused circles and meetings to keep the channels open, so that our members, when they left us, had a wide variety of knowledge and were able to work within many traditions, if they chose to. The heart of our coven was ... I was going to say 'the land', which is true in a way, but our group heart really lay in the members, as we were an intrinsic part of the land as well. And when I stopped doing all that and started my indigenous practice in a more conscious way, it was my connection to this land which was the start and (I hope) will be the very end of that.

We came together as individuals, each with our own links and our own forms of magic, we met at a structured place, a common ground. The group entity that was Crow Coven itself drew and bound us together, for a time – and what we each brought blended and connected deeper through the group, the grove, the land.

With such focus on and from our membership, it was marking our path together, through our lives and through our Craft, that was a fundamental reason for Crow Coven's very existence. Though the words, titles, and descriptions we used in our group were mostly modern terms reclaimed from historical sources, that perhaps meant quite different things to us than when they were used initially, the following ceremonies and stages of passage can still be seen, in various forms, in different types of working group, coven, community, *Clann*, or *Tuath*, the whole world over.

And I guess even more so now, since the publication and popularity of the first edition of this book from 2004 onwards.

What is Initiation?

Essentially it is a ceremony or rite of marking change and growth and/or committing you to your path. It is about experiencing a change in yourself or your life, and wanting to mark it formally, or actively doing something that you hope will bring about that change. With both of these options inevitably comes a lot of unforeseen change and growth.

In the more traditional Wiccan systems (Gardnerian and Alexandrian) we see the marking of a Witch's development in three degrees or stages. This has been accepted by most of those working in a Wiccan way; even the most eclectic recognise the need for some sort of formal recognition of your development, whether with a group or alone. We should stay aware of the fact that it is the Gods (however you perceive of them) who do the real work of initiation. This may or may not happen at your formal ritual of Initiation - though it is wonderful indeed when it does. However you have dedicated yourself to the Higher Powers of the Universe personally, it is important in a group, and even when working alone, to mark your passage through the training you undertake. This gives structure and rewards, goals, and recognised foundations on which to build the rest of our magical training.

The following are the stages that we used within Crow Coven to guide, facilitate, and formally recognise, that training and development.

Cuairteoir (Guest)

In this group, we had an initial guest period. You were accepted as a *Cuairteoir* (pron. Coor-thore), which meant 'visitor' of Crow Coven. This was for a period of a year and a day, designed to see if the potential initiate was serious about attendance and capable of working alone – not just wanting to get their Witchcraft and personal development handed to them on a plate, nor be part of some perceived clique or social club. There were rare times when this full period was not necessary - for example if a *Cuairteoir* was exceptionally skilled, well-read and personally developed before coming to us, or had worked previously in another magical group who had taken care of similar preliminary work and training. In this sort of case, they and we would have had a fair idea of what to expect, and the year and a day instead consisted of as long as it took to assure each party that they were what they claimed to be. That sussing each other out period may actually have lasted the full time anyway, and no harm to that (there was never a rush on our part, and we were instantly suspicious of anyone who was over eager to start building up degrees or scaling a perceived hierarchy), or it sometimes only lasted a few months.

Generally speaking, however, we learned from experience that this period is vital, and if it is skipped for some reason it can lead to some pretty disastrous consequences. If nothing else, it works to assure both coven and *Cuairteoir* that there will be no conflict of interest or understanding, and that all parties are mutually acceptable and won't end up duelling with wands at 20 paces. The *Cuairteoir* was a guest in every sense and was entitled to the hospitality and help of the coven throughout this time. They were not, however, entitled to a place at the hearth as yet, nor were they privy to the inner workings (certain of the meetings, instructions, or decisions of the group).

For the solitary worker, the year and a day time frame can have much relevance also. This is the time that the individual (a *'Cuairteoir'* in the sense of being a guest to the Craft) can spend reading, going to events or moots/open social meetings if they are available online or in the local area, speaking to those who are currently working Craft, or traversing the Internet and perhaps joining one of the many Social Media Groups, Chat Groups, or Forums (yes, they still exist!) that cater to those who are starting out, as well as to the more established practitioners. It is a valuable period of exploration and adjustment when you can assure yourself that this newfound path is right and good for your own development – or alternatively that it is not the way for you to go, before making any sort of formal commitment to the Craft.

We ran a system of sponsorship or mentoring during this time, which also carried on through the entire period of an individual's involvement with our group. An established group member agrees to stand as *Tacaí* (pron. Tah-Key), or 'supporter', to the *Cuairteoir*. This is - very - loosely based on the ancient Irish system of fostering: taking responsibility for the wellbeing and growth of another person who is not of your own bloodline. Within any *Tuath* (pron. Thoo-ah), or 'tribe', or a *Clann* (pron. clonn), which is a 'family', who had agreed to foster a child from outside, there may have been one of the established community members who took a special interest in the child's growth and development.

We found this useful from many angles, in a modern setting. It ensured that the group leader didn't bear the responsibility of every newcomer to the group. Of course, they could also stand as the *Tacaí* for any *Cuairteoir* – but the leader/s didn't **have** to be personally responsible for every person who came into the group, which always appealed to me when I was an over-burdened High Priestess, at least. It also enabled the newcomer to have one particular point of contact, whom they knew had willingly taken the job of looking after them - answering questions, helping them if they got stuck on anything, and even just being available as a general sounding board. Their *Tacaí* would often have been a friend first and foremost; perhaps they even introduced the person to the group in the first place, which was always helpful as a foundation. It also gave the coven leader(s) the chance to access the progress of the *Cuairteoir* independently, through reports from the *Tacaí*. Not having direct responsibility for them meant there was less chance for bias, favouritism, or clouded judgement.

If this all seems a little too formal, I can only assure you it worked (and would still work today) as a system and structure that acts more as guidelines than rigid doctrine. It may seem like overkill for a smaller group, but what it does is provide any group the space and comfort to grow without becoming overwhelmed. I go into group organisation a whole lot more in my book 'A Practical Guide to Pagan Priesthood: Community Leadership and Vocation' (Llewellyn, 2019), and this is where a lot of that began. I wouldn't have been well known back then as the most organised of High Priestesses, and this (along with some other systems and processes built in) mostly kept everything on track - but Crow Coven's membership always set the flow for the group. The structure was in place to guide rather than to rule.

After the year and a day was done, if all was to mutual satisfaction and we hadn't scared the *Cuairteoir* off in the time period of being exposed to our particular brand of madness, things were clear to move on.

NOTE: For anyone who wants to undertake an online programme of study which now covers a vast amount more than what our original Cuairteoirí would have received with Crow Coven, you can go over to the Irish Pagan School and get immediate access to over 50 courses (at time of writing, with more added each month) taught by me, through our Cuairteoir Membership.

Learn More Here - *https://irishpaganschool.com/p/guest*

Cuardaitheoir (First Stage)

The first level of commitment in our group was that of the *Cuardaitheoir* (pron. Coor DA hore), or 'seeker', which would have had roughly the equivalent of a first degree in Wicca. It signified the postulant's dedication to the group and to the tradition in which we worked. It marked the entrance of the new member to the group as a whole, committed them to us and us to them, and it stood as a declaration of intent on both parts.

Their *Tacaí* stood forth and declared them properly prepared for the role and work to follow. For the solitary practitioner, it would mark the decision to commit to the Craft for as long as is right for them to do so, to take it as far as it could be taken. It is a time to choose particular areas of study, such as what form of divination or healing they want to use, or focus more directly on areas that they had been working on previously in a general sense.

They continued at this point to learn the forms of ritual that we most often used, such as the sacred space opening and closing rituals, elemental attunement, and working in a more focused manner with land, sea, and sky (though the *Cuairteoir* would have been picking up a lot of the basics of all this too, during their initial year and a day period).

Duine Eolach (Second Stage)

The second level of commitment was that of the *Duine Eolach* (pron. Dinneh Oh-Lock) or 'learned/knowledgeable person'. This held roughly the equivalent of the second degree in traditional Wicca, and marked the passage into Priesthood; it was when the *Cuardaitheoir* became a Priest or Priestess of our tradition, entitled to teach or guide newcomers, as well as to continue learning themselves. They could, at this stage, lead and take responsibility for a circle or ritual meeting, to gain experience of such things. For solitary or group worker alike, at this point new areas of study could be chosen, new depths or heights attempted on existing talents, or particular skills honed more finely. This stage will bring particular jobs for the Priest/Priestess: they gain new responsibilities and new roles within the group. This would usually be decided based on the level of skill and commitment they had shown to developing or honing a particular talent or area of interest.

This stage also carried the new responsibility of taking on the role of *Tacaí* for a newcomer - or at least assisting or learning from an existing *Tacaí*. A solitary worker at this stage may feel ready to take the responsibility of looking to their local community for those who are just starting on the path, to guide or facilitate or support the beginning of their journey. Not to, and I must emphasise this, take on the responsibility of somebody else's training when yours has only really just begun, nor start to run a coven and perform initiations. Just to be available to warn of any dangers, help clear up any messes made, provide quality resources and recommendations, and be available as a general support person. Even in the initiatory tradition of Wicca, a second degree would only take the responsibility of another person's training under the fairly strict guidance or supervision of the original parent coven.

At this stage in your own development, whether part of a group or solitary, you may feel ready to maybe organise a local moot/meeting or social gathering, if there isn't already one in your area, or to volunteer to help out at an existing one. A study group might be possible, where those of like mind can be facilitated for meeting regularly (online or in person) to discuss books, rituals, techniques, or their own ideas and development. For solitary practitioners, the most difficult part of the path can often be the fact that there doesn't seem to be anybody to talk about your own experiences with, to ask for suggestions or help, or even just get a fresh point of view. With Craft, as with so many things in our lives, it can often be difficult to see the sacred grove for all the blooming trees that get in our way. At this point, you may feel ready to take a more active role in your local community, in whatever way you feel suits you best. Don't forget that this doesn't necessarily have to be by doing anything specifically magical. Organising tree plantings or rubbish or river clean-up, volunteering to help out at your kid's school events or the local old folks home, and a million other things, can all help to connect you to your locality and fulfill your emerging role as *Tacai*.

It happens most often that folks get to this stage and stay here for a very long time. There is no rush to move on, and much to learn from being a *Duine Eolach,* and a support person or facilitator in a group and/or in the wider community. The role of Priest or Priestess is an important one in its own right, and not ever to be treated as a mere stepping-stone on the way to a desire of being a High Priest or High Priestess, if that is a part of your path that may follow.

It has been said in many books, particularly the old school NeoPagan teachings of the 80s and 90s, that there is no clergy in Wicca/Witchcraft (as the terms are used interchangeably by those who trained and learned back then). This was true, and still is in the sense that no Craft Priest or Priestess can ever be an exclusive go-between for an individual with their Gods, such as a catholic priest would have been. Each Witch or Wiccan (or indeed, Pagan or Druid) is ultimately responsible for their own contact with the divine… though during some rituals such as 'Drawing Down the Moon', a Priestess can fulfill a certain function as a vessel for the Goddess. As such, traditional Wiccan initiations made the first degree a Priest or Priestess of the Craft.

We found this to be unhelpful in the context of the Craft we were working. There were too many eejits running around calling themselves Lady Priestess (or worse, High Priestess) Angel Fairy Raven Wolf of the Mystic Moon, based on the assumption that they had every right to call themselves a Priestess just as they liked. And look, I ran across much of the same shite - still - while writing my Pagan Priesthood book in 2018/2019. It can and will be argued that you can call yourself whatever you like, and nobody has any right to say boo to you for doing so. That, of course, is entirely true, but also extremely indicative of the sense of entitlement that has been passed down through way too many generations of imperialists and colonisers.

I was back then, and still am today, simply trying to point out that to act in such a fashion - without the sense of responsibility, experience, or training (whether from working in a group, or a thoughtful study programme of self-development work) that it takes to competently assume the role of Priesthood - you are representing modern Craft to the outside world without the skills or experience to do so. At the stage of *Duine Eolach*, or any second degree equivalent, one can at least be assured that they have spent some time living and working the tradition or path they follow, and training in a group or working diligently on their own development.

In short, the best practice here is that by the time we feel we could call a person a Priest or Priestess, they have worked hard and bloody well earned that title.

Seanóir (Third Stage)

The third stage of commitment within Crow Coven was one that few would have finally reached, to be honest. And if they did it would be after a long time as a *Duine Eolach*. Of course there were exceptions, but, generally, those who worked properly through the other stages recognised the huge element of responsibility involved in the next step, and often just wouldn't want it, or would consistently feel they weren't ready for it! Within our coven, it was that of the *Seanóir* (pron. Shan-Ore), or 'elder of the tribe'. It is roughly the equivalent to the Wiccan third degree, and marked the passage to High Priest or High Priestess. This allowed them the choice of the leadership of another group in their own right, or of continuing in our group as a coven

STAGES OF A WITCH'S LIFE

elder.

In today's eclectic Witchcraft and Wicca, the terms High Priest or High Priestess are often bandied about, mostly being used in public by those who understand the role or responsibilities the least. In the everyday course of events, you will very rarely find a genuine High Priest/ess come up to you at an event or meeting and introduce themselves as such. To the general public, it still seems to be viewed as a qualification of some sort. I suppose it is, but, without the experience and understanding behind it, it is as empty as if I declared myself the queen of all Ireland and proceeded to erect a throne in my front garden. Not having earned the right or the recognition in my chosen field (in this example, the Island of Ireland as a whole) and not being recognised by my chosen people, I would be a long time sitting on my fancy chair waiting for the subjects to start flocking to visit and beg my wisdom. Likewise, unless you have earned the right or the recognition of your chosen field, and unless you are recognised by your chosen community, you will be a long time trying to gain any respect or credibility with any sort of High Priesthood.

And I don't mean in any way that you could or should just fleet your way through three degrees of Wiccan initiations with anybody who will take you on. Those people are out there, often charging for what they call initiations, or just handing them out freely and carelessly because they are looking to build an ego boosting stable of initiates. Unfortunately, this problem hasn't gotten much better in the time between writing the first and second editions of this book. Actually going through the ceremonies is necessary of course, but, I am sad to say, some covens will still take anybody through their doors, pretty much no questions asked, and either charge for degrees or else just dole them out like smarties, as some sort of power trip for the coven leaders and a collection of empty and hollow memories for the participants.

Becoming a Priest in such a fashion means nothing. Sorry, I tell a lie, it does mean something: it means you are at best a fool, and at worst a selfish, power-hungry fool, and the ones who have 'initiated' you are reprehensible fools. The Craft is not a game, it's not a scorecard to collect titles on, nor a bedpost for your notches - and it's not some sort of elite social club that

147

you need to hold the proper rank to gain entrance to. It is for everyone who genuinely wants it, whose will is to improve themselves and the world around them, by their actions, responsibilities, experience, and knowledge. These are all words you are hearing me repeat over and over and over again. If you have noticed this, how I keep coming back to personal responsibility, then good. That is the key. And again, Personal Responsibility: responsibility for the self, and for your own actions. For your life. For your personality. For your situation. There are always choices, even if they are difficult ones. Honesty. Respect - for yourself, your own path, and that of those around you. Other people's rights to be who and what they naturally and essentially are on a fundamental level, doing what they are truly meant to be doing. If they are interfering with your right to be who and what you are truly meant to be - well then, by all means, kick them hard. If they are not, leave them alone!

That goes just as much for you as for anybody else. Your own strength is the key to being able to fulfill your role in this world. Your happiness and comfort are as important as that of anybody else. I first wrote those words as a mother of young children, who would often sacrifice my own comfort, safety, or happiness for that of my kids. But that was by choice and responsibility, not by duty, and it made me happy, not unhappy, to do so - in the long run at least - I am no martyr! I grumbled and moaned about how hard it was, as much as the next mother of young children. But I did it, stuck with my ethics and ideals and principles stubbornly through many, many adversities, and my (three) children - and new 2020 grandchild! - are a credit and a testament to that, as well as each being amazing humans in their own right..

What does all this have to do with becoming or living as a *Seanóir*? Understanding of responsibility, on a deep and fundamental level. In a group, one of the key elements in deciding who is ready for a role of such responsibility is looking at who feels they are ready for it or not. Generally, and this has far-reaching implications in the world at large, those who want or actively seek power are the last ones who should get it. One only has to look at most politicians to see the horrible truth in this statement. And by the Gods is this truer than ever for the second edition of this book, than it even was for the first.

The role of *Seanóir* is mainly that of teacher, adviser, and guide, both to other coven members and to the coven leaders themselves. The role is also, however, that of a student (as indeed are all roles within the group): we **never** stop learning and growing. Each new member changes the group's energy and its dynamics, and also brings new knowledge and experience to the collective that we can (and should) all continue to learn from. The concept of mastery also comes into play here too. All of those skills and talents we have been working on and developing through the different stages? Here is where we really focus in on one or two of them, and get truly fucking good at it. There's a lot of learning and practice involved there too, on the path to expertise.

In our group, becoming a *Seanóir* was different from becoming a High Priest or High Priestess. The latter would come with the *Seanóir* leaving our group to form their own, and if they chose to take on those titles at that point, good for them. Of course, once they gained their third-degree equivalent, they would be perfectly entitled to refer to themselves if and when it was appropriate to do so, as a High Priest or High Priestess. This self reference though, as I have already pointed out, happened quite rarely in the everyday world.

For those working alone, there will be no graduation within a group, nobody to tell them that they are ready to take the role and responsibility of *Seanóir*. It is one of the most difficult assessments to make on oneself. Often solitary workers will wait until a group of students begin to collect around them before they will take up the role or the title. Without the position of teaching and learning from students and seekers, the titles of High Priesthood, or *Seanóir,* are all a bit pointless, unless they are bestowed on you by the wider community through word or action. There are many in our Irish community who do not teach formally, do not run groups, and have never followed any official form of training or initiations. Yet when I speak to them, I am in no doubt that the respect due to any *Seanóir* is theirs for the taking, though they rarely look for or expect it. Elder of the tribe or

149

Seanóir is particularly appropriate in such cases, as they work to serve the wider community with grace and inherent responsibility, and a mischievous (or necessary) poke with a sharp stick every so often.

Irish Rites of Passage

In Ireland, we can see some very distinct stages in a person's life. As the majority of the country is still not just christian, but Roman catholic (though the church's monopoly is visibly loosening year by year), the stages are still being marked in this context. But if we examine them, we can see that the people still have similar markers of our life's progress that we have always had, regardless of what religion holds sway.

In the following, we examine the stages as they stand, and I am generalising - I must stress. Not all families follow this pattern to the letter; not all families are the stereotypical Irish drinkers or catholics. But these traditions are carried on in most schools (we have, as yet, no separation of church and state), and therefore in most lives throughout the country. You might wonder why I am examining the traditions of the christian religion, but, as you will see, it is all a part of being Irish!

Irish Paganism is a living, organically growing, syncretic blend - a lot of our current social traditions are only the modern form of the much older Pagan ways of reckoning, and they still run a lot deeper in the national culture and psyche than just religious observance.

A Note to the 2nd Edition: I've left a lot of the following as is, feeling it will be useful for many still. The basic christian spiritual practice which has nativised here, and the people who hold these beliefs in good faith, deserve and receive my respect and my blessing. I have to be clear though, that since writing the 1st edition I've had a geis or sacred restriction put upon me, by my Gods, that I am forbidden from participating in or even energetically supporting any service or ceremony conducted in the name of the criminal cult that calls itself the catholic 'church' in Ireland. This means I have missed the christening, wedding, and funeral ceremonies of those very near and dear to me, including my own dearest Nana. I support those people, and respect their choices if they are made clearly and not blindly or routinely. However, the crimes of the organisation they bind themselves and their children to, crimes against our people and our land, run deep; and there are many travesties that even yet remain uncovered, festering and spreading poison beneath the surface of our society. I do not recognise their authority in Ireland, and I reject their doctrine and their criminal organisation in every way. It is my heartfelt wish and my prayer that the rest of my people will follow suit, some day.

The Christening is held when a child is but a few weeks old. In Ireland, this generally means the family getting together, ostensibly to dedicate the new life to the church, but in reality to have a right old natter and knees-up. The child is dressed in fine robes (often in robes made of the mother's wedding dress, signifying the continuing cycle and family connection) and usually a bonnet or cap handmade by the granny. It may be a bonnet sewn from a linen hanky that had been given as a wedding gift. All the aunties bring cakes and dishes, everybody brings a bottle – the party starts at the gates of the church and finishes in the wee small hours with Uncle Packy being politely but firmly shown the door.

In this, we see the **Celebration of Birth**, where a child is presented to the Gods and the *clann*, accepted by the priest and by the community and formally given his name. Guardians are chosen in the form of 'Godparents': those who will take responsibility for and guide the child should anything happen to his parents. The new life is celebrated with copious feasting and drinking, and some singing too if you are very unlucky.

First Holy Communion happens at around age 7. This occasion has a big deal made of it in schools. It is the first time a child is allowed to take the 'Communion' with their God, in the form of wafers in the church. The girls dress up in white frilly dresses and the boys in smart suits. They accept responsibility for the first time for their own spirituality, theoretically at least: with first confession (to 'cleanse' them), then the communion with the

151

'body of Christ'.

Here we see the **Age of Reason** ceremony, where a child is for the first time able to make connections and accept the consequences of his spiritual decisions. This may seem quite heavy for a 7 year old, but it is a celebration and a time to meet deity or start forming relationships, to start thinking about the Universe beyond the bounds of the normal, rather than just the immediate concerns of Dora the Explorer and which one of Bob the Builder's machinery friends would win if they had a race (I'm leaving those rather dated references in, because anything I change them to will no doubt quickly go out of fashion too!). I must stress that it is a start; no child reaching their age of reason (and this is different for each individual; in Pagan terms, we go by the personality rather than the physical age) is expected to be suddenly mature and completely self-aware.

Confirmation occurs around the age of 12, just before they move from junior school (primary) to senior school (secondary). This is supposed to be a literal confirmation of the vows taken by the parents for the child at christening: Do you believe in God, Jesus, and the evil of the Devil? Not many people I know actually believed all this stuff, but they got the fancy new clothes, said they did, and then got money for their troubles from each relative and neighbour.

This coincides with the **Reaching of Puberty**. It is a time to celebrate the child coming into a more adult stage in their life – their physical body changing, developing, and growing in preparation for the later responsibilities of sexual exploration and possibly having their own children. Further responsibility is now taken for their own development; they are getting more grown-up all the time. The supposed purity of the confirmation age has taken much of the older celebration of developing sexuality, sanitised it, and cut us off from a celebration of our own body and its burgeoning natural gifts. The unhealthy consequences of this can be seen throughout not just Ireland, but in most of Western society.

There are a few celebrations upon reaching adulthood in Ireland, but they are generally grouped under one heading or time frame in a person's life - the period where they are leaving the school system and moving into the adult world. There is the 18th birthday party, the graduation (from school) party, and a big dance celebration called the Debs, which usually happens around the time we get the results of our final exam: the Leaving Certificate. The 21st birthday party, which is the main one really, is the climax of these and marks the official 'handing over the keys of the door', which is for practicality's sake now done in actuality a lot earlier, but traditionally the youngster would not have gained the freedom of the house, to come and go as they pleased, until their 21st.

This stage is the **Celebration of Adulthood**, a time when the young person reaches the final independence of their parents and may strike out on their own. In our terms, it can be marked at various times, from an actual event such as a person moving into their own place for the first time, to a more general 'I trust you to take responsibility for yourself now' ceremony. Responsibility for your own actions is the key to this time.

Marriage is the stage traditionally where a father lets his daughter go into the keeping of his new son-in-law. He literally gives away the bride, as if she was still his property - creepy when you think about it like that, huh?! Nevertheless, it is obviously a big celebration in any family, in many cases it will be one of the biggest and best feasts we put on in our lifetime. There aren't any dowries as such anymore, but traditionally the bride's father would have paid for the wedding. Practically, these days, it is the couple themselves who pay for most of it!

This is equivalent to our **Handfasting Ceremony**, the voluntary joining of a couple, where two separate paths blend to one - for as long as that is right for both parties - and the beginning of the circle of a new family unity.

There are many ways to mark the rest of a couple's lives together, from the renewal of vows many years on, to big 20th, 40th, or even 50th anniversary parties. Often the couple will hold an anniversary or renewal party, or even both together, after a particular stage in their marriage, such as all the kids

153

leaving home or a rough patch they have made it through.

This is the **Strengthening of Ties**, where a married couple refreshes and renews themselves, re-committing to their continuing love for one another, and deciding to stay on their joint pathway together, for the foreseeable future.

For one reason or another, whether through the loss of a loved one, a parting of the ways for a couple, retirement from work, or simply a personal journey that leads to finding oneself, there is sometimes a need to celebrate being yourself, and being happy with that. With rising marital separation and divorce figures (not such a taboo subject here anymore, thankfully), this is ever on the increase and should not be ignored. We see it coming through in many forms in modem Irish society - both in genuinely unhealthy mid-life crises, and in healthier expressions of comfort and joy in who we are. A common one now is the middle-aged woman who has come into her own. This may be through a separation, the sudden freedom as the last child leaves the nest, or just a realisation that mother and housewife are not all she is, nor all she ever has to be.

Traditionally in Irish society, men have had much more freedom from the home and personal liberty than women, but all of that is changing. So now we see things such as divorce parties, and older people getting pierced, tanned, and tattooed, dressing more in line with current fashions - generally enjoying their lives a lot more and being proud of themselves and their achievements. Some view these things as a mid-life crisis, which can have awfully negative connotations and be used to dismiss a person's genuine need to express themselves more fully or make necessary changes - until they either break free or give it up.

As this is a relatively new phenomenon here, there isn't really an Irish Pagan equivalent, other than the constant affirmation of life and self that most Witches and Pagans engage in! But I feel it is an important movement within our culture, so I have chosen to mark it too. I call it the **Coming of Age**, to signify a person's prime of life, whatever their physical age or circumstances. It is that stage when you realise you can live wholly for you, be yourself, and continue to grow, learn, and blossom.

Ireland is one of the few modern cultures to still truly celebrate a funeral as a life that has passed to death. We refer to part of the process as a Wake, where family and friends get together and stand vigil over the person who has passed; they are never left alone from the time of death to that of burial. My own Granda was buried in his true heart's home in County Clare, in the West of Ireland, though he died in Dublin in the East. While travelling to his burial, we stopped at one of his favourite pubs for sandwiches and drinks, and for them to say goodbye too. We had somebody stay outside with him the whole time, and quite a few whiskeys were raised in his honour after being shuffled from pub to path. The party that was held to celebrate his life is one that village didn't forget in a hurry. The Wake is a time for remembering and honouring the person's life and their achievements. The funeral service (usually a mass in the church beside the graveyard or crematorium) and the burial or cremation practice follow on from this.

This rite has been named the Requiem in various Wiccan-based books, but I prefer the **Rite of Passing**, the literal and final passage of a person's body, until the next turnabout of their soul's cycle. It is a time to say goodbye to this incarnation on the continuing journey of life, death, and rebirth - and of course to celebrate the life they have lived, and their contributions to your own life. It marks a passing and an end to one way, but the beginning of another is always promised and present.

Irish Pagan Alternatives

Now we look to the rituals and rites we can use to mark these stages, common in practically every Irish person's lifetime, but based on that syncretic blend of much older traditions and our modern Irish culture... so we can see how the Irish Witch of today can mark their path and that of their family's.

The topics covered are as laid out previously, providing an alternative to Irish (catholic) culture, while keeping within its more valid traditions.

Catholicism is viewed by many christians as a form of Witchcraft in itself, with the candles and incense and 'Goddess' veneration - the Virgin Mary. What is found in Ireland today has, at the very least, echoes of our Pagan past. For those of us raising families in Ireland, it will also be useful for integration of ourselves and our children into Irish culture, while also staying true to the needs and rites of our spiritual selves.

Celebration of Birth

Fáilte Romhat (pron. Fawl-tyah Roe-ath). This Irish greeting, given when bidding a person welcome, literally means 'Welcome to You'. Elements of the ritual here would include:

- Giving the child their name/names - every day, and a magical name if that is appropriate.
- Official acceptance of them into the *Clann* (family) by using and recognising their *Clann* name (surname), in front of the *Tuath* (tribe) or community.
- Consecration of the child; a blessing for them with oil, water, wine, or earth of the family's land. Note - this is a gift in the form of the formal blessing of an already sacred body, not a cleansing of any sort.
- Guardians in the form of Godparents or a *Caomhnóir* (pron. Kweev-Nore), 'Guardian, Protector, Patron' step up and take responsibility for whatever aspects of the child's life or development that has been previously agreed with the parent(s).
- The child is shown - physically presented, raised, or brought around to any of - the World, Water, and Sky, the four Quarters or five Provinces, the Sun/Moon/Stars - and to the people present.

Age of Reason

In this rite, a day out or some form of treat can be necessary, as the child may be feeling left out if their friends are getting spoiled at their Communion! The treat or special day should also include some space and time, perhaps a walk, with a one-on-one talk between the child and parent(s), and a new suit of clothes in a more mature style than is usual (the modern equivalent of graduating from short pants to long!). This should facilitate and support the child's dawning understanding of themselves as more grown-up than before.

A gathering of friends and family in the home would be an appropriate treat to mark this occasion; with a party or celebration theme and mood, and the child as the centre of attention in a positive way.

Reaching of Puberty

For obvious reasons, this can be an awkward one. Any young person may be uncomfortable about their body's changes, for all sorts of reasons. It's worth a mention and a check in here - physical sex and gender identity are different things, and it could be around this time that any disparity between what's visible on the outside, and what is felt and understood on the inside, may become apparent. If you have any inclination that a child in your care may be having these feelings, and you're not sure how to handle that yourself, PLEASE seek professional advice from LGBTQ aligned organisations who do this sort of support work. There are so many resources available now. Use them.

If appropriate (see above, and please be as certain as you can be), it may be an idea to hold this space for the young person with just people who identify as women, or just people who identify as men. For a young girl, this could involve a gathering of female presenting family members, and for a young boy, a gathering of male presenting family members. In the original edition of this book I made some suggestions that really reinforced the traditional gender roles and inclinations, and I'm removing all of that here. You do what's right for, and representative of, the women and men of your own family and friends group - and if that's an archery outing for the girls and a baking class for the boys, all well and good. Presenting them with non-toxic, non-stereotyped, healthy and happy examples of their existing role models is what is most important at this stage - both for their own development, and for the changes that we need to see within our societies.

Talking to the young person is the key here - actually, scratch that... listening to them is the most important part of this experience. Mark their changes in a comfortable and celebratory way. If done in this manner, it encourages openness in the family, especially between the parent and child.

This rite and significant time of change should not be dropped on them out of the blue. You can't display embarrassment or refuse to speak to a child about sexuality, or body parts, their whole lives - and then expect them to be amenable to the idea of suddenly embracing any of this with open arms. How you feel about such things yourself should be taken into consideration, and if you haven't been open and honest thus far with your children on these issues, perhaps some self-examination is in order, instead of forcing the potential alienation of your teenager. This ceremony should open up lines of communication for future discussions on sexual activity, contraception, relationships, and a million other things that are usually swept under the rug, especially in Ireland. Of course, the young person may not want to talk to their parent(s) about such things; teenagers are big with their privacy and are often highly embarrassed by their parents' wishes to discuss such subjects as sexuality with any frankness. That's ok, let them lead with their own consent and comfort levels. The point is that they need to know that they **can** talk to you, and that they have other trusted adults and role models available for support too.

Celebration of Adulthood

This is more likely to be marked through a series of events: end-of-school exam results, Debs or Prom parties, first time living away from the family home, going to college, and so forth. A 21st birthday is a good general one with which to mark this time. I wouldn't go doing anything the night they choose to have their party, mind you; they may not appreciate that sort of carry-on in front of invited friends and family.

When the time is right, there should be some form of formal handing over at this rite, traditionally it is the 'key of the door', but it goes much deeper than that. Whatever is handed over to the young adult at this time should represent or symbolise responsibility for oneself. The parent is handing over the responsibility for the offspring, to their own selves.

Handfasting Ceremony

Given here is an appropriate ceremony for a couple who have decided to commit to spending the rest of their lives together. There are also year and a day marriages, which may have happened at Lúnasa each year, a time of contracts. That type of ritual can be an adapted or even toned-down version of what's presented here - renewed yearly with a strengthening of ties, or released at the appropriate time, as required.

I personally don't hold with soul tying type marriages - that is, committing to spend eternity with a person. It depends on how it is done of course, and the couple's own understanding of it... but in general it just seems like a bad idea. I feel that if you have work to do together as a couple, or even in each other's lives, you will come together naturally anyway. Why bind yourself unnecessarily to one person life after life if you have nothing more to learn or teach together? Previous ties can be acknowledged, but future ones should be left as they are, without our somewhat arrogant meddling. So I have given here the usual for a lifetime commitment package.

Bearing in mind that a handfasting would usually be done with a working group, or at least with interested participants from the couple's friends and family helping out as part of the ceremony, elements of the ritual here would include:

- The couple is left outside whatever sacred space is set up, initially.
- The couple is questioned, and made to state their names formally, then anointed and consecrated with oil (we used our coven oil to link them as guests of our group and our grove), and they step forward of their own free will together into the space.
- The three powers of World, Water, and Sky are introduced to the ceremony, and thus to the couple. Whatever these things symbolise for the couple or the group, are brought into the mix, as an invocation of their powers and a blessing for the couple's union. World, Land, Earth can represent the steadfast, growth, or the home. Water, Sea can represent the depth of emotion shared, desire, and a multi-lifetime relationship or wish for eternity together. Sky can represent a meeting of the minds, the will, and choice to join together, or the resolve of commitment. Of course, anything appropriate to the couple may be added here; whatever significantly represents the powers of World, Water, and Sky to them should be brought forth here. In a more Wiccan or ceremonial magical setting, this would be representations of the four Elements.
- The couple exchanges their vows. In every handfasting I ever work on, the couple writes their own vows. This is essential. The vows should be promises to each other, and themselves, for the future. They should be mutual contractual obligations that are being made clear. They should be expressions of the shared love and reminders of why they are committing to each other. Ideally, they should be as mushily romantic as possible so you can make the Priest cry. That's always good for a laugh.
- Exchange of the circle of unity. This can be represented by rings, bracelets, necklaces, woven belts, crowns... anything that is circle-shaped. Please note: Claddagh rings are not essential, and are not as

essentially Irish as you might have been led to believe. It should be made clear here that *an Fáinne* (pron. On Fawn-ya), 'the Ring/circle', represents many things. It is the circle and support of family. It is the cycle of life, death, and rebirth. It is free-flowing unity, unending, unbroken.

- The binding of the couple's hands, the literal *Lámha Ceangail* ('hand binding/tying'), or handfasting. Each will have brought their own cord or rope to the ceremony, as individuals. Their hands are tied separately at first, each with their own cord. Both cords are then used to bind both hands together: a coming together of individuals as one united entity, though each with their own unique part in that.

- At this point, any poetry, quotation, or song can be introduced, usually from the couple's friends and family as gifts and blessings.

- Formal recognition of the couple's unity - and an entreaty placed on all present (both physically and not so physically) to see, know, and remember what has happened that day. This is to recognise the couple as married in the eyes of all and the Universe, and to charge all who are present to recognise and remember this in all future dealings.

- The couple then moves from their old life to their new - traditionally this is done by jumping the broomstick (which also represents a sweeping away of their old lives), but can be done by any formal stepping process, over a staff or a stick, jumping the fire, or wending through a bower decorated with seasonal flowers. Their hands are still bound at this stage, as they move forward together.

- They also celebrate their union together by cutting their food (a three-tiered wedding cake is nice, but we have also used an apple) and drinking something from a shared cup, with hands still bound. The bonds can come off after this; everybody will have gotten the picture by that point I'm sure.

After all this, it's party time. Live music, marquees, grandmothers chatting to coveners, finger and buffet food with vegans wondering what they can eat, drinking (lots of drinking), dancing, fire walking - I've seen it all (and who could ever forget a hung-over *buachaill bocht* with a bag of frozen peas

161

on his burnt feet the morning after a failed fire walk?! Don't do that). The traditional Irish wedding rows with Aunty Mary we could probably do without. Other than that, it's all good, so enjoy your celebrations.

Strengthening of Ties

Anything relevant for a handfasting is relevant for strengthening or refreshing the bonds between a couple. A gathering and celebration is a good idea, especially with as many of the original cast and crew from your handfasting as possible. In this way everybody's promise to see, know, and remember is refreshed. The couple also gets to express their continuing love for each other, and their continuing commitment to their *Clann*, by restating their vows. And you get to have another party.

Coming of Age

Do a parachute jump. Tour India. Get a tattoo. Get a divorce. Get a snake. Make it as personal or as public as you like. This is a time for re-examination and reclamation. A stock take on how close who you have become really is to who you want to be. Read old diaries; dig out your old yearbooks or your first CV or college prospectus. Really think about who you wanted to be, what you wanted to make of your life. Some of your original dreams and goals will have changed for the better and matured. But some of them will have been cast aside in favour of duty or responsibility, fear, or plain old laziness. It is not too late, as long as you draw breath. This is the time to be honest, and brave. To paraphrase both Franklin D. Roosevelt and Nelson Mandela: Courage is not the absence of fear; it is the ability to overcome it.

Rite of Passing

Slán Abhaile (pron. Slawn Ah-wal-ya). This Irish parting, given when wishing a person safe journey, literally means 'Safe Home'. This ceremony will be necessarily personal to the family of the deceased. If it is a case where the person and their family was this way inclined, one can go the whole hog: plaster the place with triple spirals (an Irish image of three merged spirals; perhaps symbolising life, death, and rebirth), mourn the passing of a friend or family member, but celebrate their time of well-deserved rest and imminent return.

In Ireland, we used to hire professional Keeners to come and cry at funerals. A *caoin* (pron. keen) is a cry or lament. The hiring of professionals probably started with the village biddys wailing over the bodies of the more popular folks, and everybody's family wanted it known that they would be missed. The biddys then found themselves with a commercially viable talent. There are connections here (I suppose) to the lore of the *Bean Sidhe* - a family's ancestral spirit could be called in to take the person's spirit safely away with her, by mimicking her cry.

As mentioned earlier, from the time of passing, the person's body is never left alone. There is always a friend or family member on hand - or in the case of necessary funeral administration, at least a funeral home official. This is the origin of the Wake: that a waking vigil is kept until the body is laid to rest. It has denigrated somewhat to mean the party of the funeral, the drinking session, but this is only the celebratory part of the process.

If a ceremony is appropriate or feasible, the celebrant should ideally be someone quite well known to the deceased. Elements of the ceremony could include, as much as possible:

- Remembering the name of the person who has passed, recognition of their titles and accomplishments, their honours and commitments through life. Detailing what their name meant to those left behind, the associations and impressions still felt upon hearing that name.
- An official remembrance of them from a *Clann* (family) official or repre-

sentative, listing their contributions to the family and the community as a whole, in front of the *Tuath* (tribe) or community.

- Consecration of the person's body, a blessing for them with oil, water, wine, or earth of the family's land.
- Remembering the person to the World, Water, and Sky - and also to the four Provinces or quarters/directions of Ireland, with the sacred centre (so, five in all) - and to the people present.
- During any of this it is appropriate that those actually involved, friends and family, speak about the person who has passed... not just the celebrant. If the person didn't leave any specific wishes, it is really up to the family what they would like to see. Things such as favourite music, poetry, and discussion can all be an integral part of the letting-go process. There should also be frequent reminders throughout, of the cyclical nature of life, death, and rebirth. The triple spiral is an image that will speak volumes at this time.

And then the obligatory party: the funeral session in which the person's life and contributions are celebrated and many a glass raised in their honour. There will be a sad note, of course, but always a reminder of life within death. I actually got engaged at my Granda's funeral party... it wasn't planned, but it was very appropriate. I am the eldest granddaughter, and it marked a new chapter of his family's history opening up.

There is also a tradition in most parts of Ireland to have the Month's Mind. This is a remembrance mass held one month after the funeral. I have always felt it gave the family and friends an opportunity to get together again, see how each is doing, and then just get on with their lives as best they can, after it. To give some closure and comfort. It is something to think about at least, and perhaps adapt for your own use.

Whether celebrating your life and your magic alone or in a group - I wish you well. Marking the stages as you develop and grow gives tremendous satisfaction, and a sense of accomplishment and achievement that makes it a very worthwhile endeavour.

Beir Bua 's Beannacht!

III

How It Will Be

7

To Conclude

With all this talk about the integration of magic in Irish culture, how the beliefs are embedded and the Pagan traditions enshrined in everyday use on this fair and lovely isle, you, Dear Reader, would be forgiven if you were to believe that on your first visit to Ireland, you could justifiably walk right up to any common or garden Irish citizen and (politely) demand to be pointed in the direction of the local Pagans, please.

Well, that's not quite the thing to do.

Although the Irish Gaels are a very powerful people, and our land is filled to the brim with magic and mystery, most of us don't actually know this, on any conscious day-to-day level at least. It may be easy enough to spot from the outside, or for a student of modern magic to pick through and examine, but, for your aforementioned common or garden Irish citizen, we are still a predominantly catholic country, and there are no two ways about it. This stuff is normal and natural to us, but mostly subconscious and so embedded into our upbringing and culture that it goes largely unnoticed and unremarked.

So if you approach Paddy Joe the farmer in a local pub somewhere in Connacht on a Friday evening and inquire as to the whereabouts of the nearest moot, the nearest fairy tree, the nearest Witch or healer, you will most likely be met with a blank stare and a muttered comment along the lines of, 'Well, I wouldn't know about that now'. He will then shuffle off to the other end of the bar to discuss the price of heifers with Micky Joe (the other farmer). If you happen to meet a particularly friendly and intelligent Paddy Joe, he might rub his chin first, chew his pipe, and have a bit of a think for you, but probably the end result will be the same.

Modern ideas of Paganism or Witchcraft haven't penetrated very deeply into rural Ireland even now; a Witch would still be (if given any thought at all) a woman who could probably hex your cows. This is true enough of course, but the point being that the likes of Charmed or Buffy the Vampire Slayer (or Sabrina, for a slightly more recent update at time of writing the second edition) won't have made it onto your average Paddy Joe's TV screen. They probably won't have been online recently to check on the doings of the Irish Pagan community, nor will they be overly familiar with modern organisations such as Pagan Life Rites (Ireland). In short, they most likely won't have a bloody clue what you are talking about.

There are, of course, exceptions to every rule. As modern Paganism, Wicca, Shamanistic practices, Druidry, and Witchcraft continue to grow in strength and numbers, things do filter down in some ways. We have had an influx of 'New Age hippies' (as they are fondly referred to in the communities) into the South and West of Ireland primarily. By hippies they mean foreign sorts - English, Americans, Danish, Germans, and the rest - who have decided that this land is their spiritual and tranquil home and they want to spend the rest of their days living quietly on some smallholding around here, with maybe a goat or two and the odd chicken for company (which all sounds good to me, and fair play to them for doing it). Incomers such as this are still thought of as weirdos certainly, for the most part, but with a certain relaxation of prejudice that is fairly unique to the Irish. Once they settle in and start to participate in the community, though they may always be thought of as weirdos, they will generally come to be viewed as our weirdos. These hippies are viewed as tourists more than anything, and as such are given the normal *céad mile fáilte* ('a hundred thousand welcomes') and warm reception. Visit your local pub with any regularity and you will not be short of company or an ear to bend.

In the Pub

Speaking of, you can hear some strange things down the pubs here. The following may be of interest to anybody who is considering a move to rural Ireland. A lot of folks I speak to would love to live the dream of moving here, but (among other, more practical issues) are afraid of how they will be viewed or reacted to by locals. In a little rural village in East Clare, in one of the local pubs that you end up entering because it's the only place serving anything resembling food on a rainy Sunday afternoon, I came across the most amazing discussion as I sat and quietly ate my soggy chips and wrinkly sausages. On my arrival, there had just been the obligatory line of Sunday drinkers along the bar: old men who get up, get dressed, maybe go to Mass, and then spend all day propping up the bar. About halfway through my meal, the daughter-in-law of one of the men came in to join him for a drink. They got to talking, and it turned out she was English (originally, but even being married to an Irish person doesn't rid you of the English tag entirely) and an amateur herbalist of sorts (interested in making up her own cures and remedies, at least). The father-in-law seemed like he had been aware of this for a while, and was going on about the things she had fixed for him with her remedies. He seemed fairly proud of her, actually. I kept quiet and kept eating, to hear what the reaction from the other old men and the slightly disapproving matron behind the bar would be. At the time, I was considering moving to the area myself, and had put an offer in on a house nearby. As I would in effect be the newest local Witch if that house sale went through, I had more than a passing interest in the conversation going on at the bar.

And it was interesting indeed. One of the men piped up, though obviously embarrassed enough, and asked her if there was anything she could recommend for difficulties with his urination. He didn't phrase it quite so politely, mind you. Her advice seemed sound enough to me, and included directions to see the doctor immediately should symptoms persist. The fact that a local farmer could (relatively) casually ask a weirdo English girl for such a herbal treatment for a personal and sensitive issue, in a public bar, was very encouraging to me while considering my move to a supposedly backward country area, from a busy Irish City. Things are coming on in Ireland, and we're opening up. Slowly, but surely still, we are opening.

In the School

While we are on the subject of moving to a rural Irish community, whether you are coming from one of the larger Irish cities or from another country altogether (as I am sure lots of you who are reading this book will have at least considered doing, at some stage or another)... a bigger worry I have come across than local reaction to them personally, from those considering the move, has been schooling for their kids. Being the mother of two very young children at the time, it was also a huge concern of mine. Catholicism in Ireland is still quite stubbornly dug in - yes, even in second edition times! Things are changing, and we have definitely made even more progress, but slowly. I cannot, of course, speak for every person's troubles or joys on making this move. All I can do is share my own experiences.

My kids were not raised christian or catholic, as I knew a lot of Irish Pagans were doing, so as "not to make life tough" for their kids. The reality of doing such a thing is, I always felt and still do, setting up a very hypocritical and confusing situation for the children. As a Pagan and a Witch, I felt that raising my kids as christians would be telling them that being Paganism is somehow not okay. It would send the message to them that christianity is better, as it's the done thing, and it's somehow preferred and even expected of them to conform, pretend, and try your best to fit in.

To be clear, I wasn't raising them specifically as Pagan either; just answering questions openly as and when they cropped up naturally from the children. I was open about my own spirituality, they could always see how important that was to me, and I never had any problems with doing things that way (until their formerly Pagan - I presume he gave up on that spirituality when he forswore his initiatory oaths to betray a fellow of the Craft?! - father tried to use it all against me in Court, including bringing an original copy of this book to the custody trial… but that's a whole other story!). My kids have grown up to be amazing, wonderful, loving humans (though I am sure every mother thinks that of her own children!). And it's not just our family. Anybody raising their kids sensibly in a Pagan household, whether in Ireland or America or anywhere else, will have the same results.

Sensibly is the key here; some Pagan parents are honestly just flakes, and use Paganism as an excuse not to discipline their children and to let them roam free under the pretense of home schooling so as to avoid the catholic held school system. All of which is a recipe for utter disaster, in my opinion. I know many non christian kids now who have been fully through the Irish school system, start to finish, their parents having pointed out to the school authorities from the start that they were not being raised as catholic. Simple as that. While there are occasional battles to be fought, depending on the individual school and management, I haven't found it to be any more so than I would expect from raising kids anywhere else outside the norm.

Your child's religion, or lack of organised religion, is really nobody else's concern, and most folks these days recognise and respect that. It's up to the parent how ostracised the child is going to be. If you are adamant that your children will not be 'polluted' by christian doctrine in any way, then they will need to sit outside the classroom for some of the day in most Irish schools. I never had a problem with my children voluntarily participating in what the other kids learned at their catholic schools. It is mostly about the teachings of Jesus, and that's not bad stuff really, at the end of the day. When there came a time that one or another of them specifically didn't want to participate, that's fine, too. It was entirely their choice, and I backed them up through every step. The only thing I was very firm about was that they didn't ever go through the ceremonies of communion or confirmation, never having been christened. I marked their path through life as much as they were comfortable with, but I didn't want any religion imposed upon them officially until they were well and truly old enough to make their own choices, whether that turned out to be catholicism, Paganism, or anything else.

In the Community

If you move to Ireland, what will people's reaction to you be? When we moved to Roscommon, I had no idea how the local community would react to me as an openly Pagan Witch - or even as someone from Dublin. The Jackeens, as we have been called, aren't generally to be trusted by many country folk here. Of course, I needn't have worried; the community welcomed us with interest and warmth. If they kept their distance slightly it was more due to the fact, I am sure, that I was quite a bit younger than most of my new neighbours than to the fact that I was from Dublin. As I arrived alone with two young children, a few of them were also a bit concerned that I might be a single mother, which was still a bit of a taboo around there, I am afraid. As they quickly realised I was in fact married (though he worked away), well, that was all right then.

Saying that, I must point out that this was my perceived reaction from one or two of the older churchgoing ladies in the vicinity, I am also quite sure that the majority of my neighbours at the time wouldn't have given a shit if I was alone or if I had three husbands in tow. I carried quite a bit of unnecessary paranoia with me when I arrived. I was waiting for the outcry or the accusations, the unfriendliness, the sly looks or whispered gossip, and it never happened!

Except for that one time a disgusting local career politician good oul boy decided that running a Goddess festival from the Heritage Centre in Tulsk (which I was the Manager of) was bad for the area, despite the national press attention, ringing pub and restaurant tills, and full to capacity local accommodation. It was bad because... Witchcraft. Go figure?!

From the start though, I approached the 'I am open as a Pagan Witch' potential problem the same way I always did: with a degree of common sense, and no need to fly the flag or change the world right out the gate. If asked directly, I was always open and honest, but unless it came up naturally in conversation, there was absolutely no need to make the point that I was a Witch. It was nobody's business but my own. If I was speaking to somebody who didn't have the interest or the intelligence to ask about me or to guess or wonder about me, then I wasn't going to share such a personal and important part of my life with them. During the course of the first year, it happened to come up naturally only three times.

The first was with a woman I had grown friendly with. She visited our house often. She casually mentioned religion and beliefs quite a few times, probably as she had noticed (and was curious about) the piles of Witchcraft books, magazines, artefacts, ritual tools, and ornaments that peppered my house! She knew I wasn't catholic; I was quite open about that as it comes up more often in this society where catholicism is so prevalent. That had been addressed when she offered me her daughter's communion dress to keep for one of mine; I just said mine wouldn't be making their communions as we aren't catholic, and left it at that. The little hints and openings were happening more regularly, and she must have been getting more and more curious but thought it rude to ask outright. Eventually, when we spoke of my writing work, I suggested there was a book in the offing, and she asked directly what it would be about. So I told her, and, after a few initial questions that had been bugging her, her attitude was just - fair enough, your beliefs are your beliefs. When I suggested that some folks would be less than pleased about it, might even not want to be friends with me after hearing such a thing, she simply said, "If they don't accept you for what you are, there is no reason to have them in your life anyway". That was me told!

The second and third times were similar circumstances. There were questions about my children's schooling, which led to me asking questions about which school had more relaxed religious policies, leading to more questioning of our situation. I admitted I wasn't catholic, nor were my kids, and discussed my interest in Irish history, pre-christian beliefs, deity, and mythology. The W-word was not mentioned either time, but that's okay. If they don't ask outright, then they don't need to know.

It is difficult to this day to balance my own desire to teach and educate people about Paganism, and my instincts to help open other folks to an awareness of their own spirituality, with the need to be relatively circumspect and responsible. It was even more so while having to be sensitive to my children and the environment they were growing up in. I wanted to shout it from the rooftops - how wonderful this choice of religion and lifestyle makes me feel every day. I wanted everyone to give up the patriarchy and the fighting and the toxic festering criminal cult... and just follow their own hearts honestly and respectfully, find their true will and work in accordance with that. But that's not very practical. Each must come to these realisations in their own time.

So I, and every responsible parent and Witch in Ireland will continue to walk a fine line.

In the Irish Pagan Community

Some of those who think of themselves as modern Druids have been rather unkindly referred to as the 'bedsheet brigade'. This comes from the way they continue to dress up in white bed sheets at solstices and dance around, get drunk, then go home and put back on their suits for the office job the following morning. (Me. It was me who called them the bedsheet brigade, and it stuck.) This type of part-time Pagan does nothing to promote or help the reputation or community standing of any of us. Of course, there are many who use the term Druid in all earnestness and respect. They live their lives as they feel the Druids of old would have done and are certainly not included in the bedsheet brigade observations. But they are few and far between, I'm afraid.

Though the author of a particularly damaging book has died since this work was first written, it is a book that absolutely galls me, and is being sold and believed in to this day. So again, I must address here, what is erroneously being viewed by some as Irish Witchcraft.

'Witta' could never be "the Irish Gaelic term for the Anglo-Saxon word Wicca", as Edain McCoy wrote in her book 'Witta: an Irish Pagan Tradition'. This cannot be true, as there is no W in the Irish language, except in loan words. There are other claims: that Colcannon is an ancient sacred food (it came from America, around the 20th century), that the potato is an ancient Irish fertility symbol (when we have seen previously that it was introduced

176

to Ireland relatively recently), and more - too much more. Suffice it to say, Witta is not Irish. If you like it as a system, please know that it hasn't got anything to do with Ireland or it's magical traditions. It is appropriative commercial trash that was written in either complete and utter ignorance, or filthy unethical capitalism, and should be taken off the market immediately. In my opinion.

While we're at it, the same goes for DJ Conway's 'Celtic Magic', which is still for sale as I write this.

Another brand altogether than Wittans are the modern Celtic Reconstructionist Pagans. These are folks who seem genuinely, for the most part, interested in and concerned about historical and cultural accuracy. The phrase Celtic Reconstructionist came into common use during 1992 and 1993 to describe individuals who were looking to research and re-create an authentically Celtic path for modern Pagans. The founders researched and studied texts and languages, did work through personal journeying and artistic expression, wrote articles, and gathered enough material to create the groundwork for what they see as a modern Celtic tradition. From an article published originally on Witchvox:

> CR makes no claims to being a True and Authentic Survival of any Celtic tradition. We acknowledge fully and openly that what we are practicing are a set of modern creations, based in and inspired by early Celtic beliefs. We follow our inspiration while remaining as true as we can to the guidelines we find in early texts, the work of scholars and archaeologists, and the practical aspects of what works well for us. CR is a constantly growing and evolving path, seeking learning, mystic and ecstatic experience, and the intense life of the spirit.

This is not the Irish Paganism I practice and now teach - mine is the organic growth of a living tradition, strongly rooted in native soil and spirit... though we do share similarly in seeking the guidance of early texts, and inspiration from the work of scholars and archaeologists, which should never be ignored.

There are of course NeoPagan covens and witchcraft groups working in Ireland, both traditional Wicca and more eclectic forms. There are those who claim family traditions of Witchcraft, who work with magic as a force of this world and the Other. There are many solitary seekers and quite a few loosely organized events that take place around the Sabbats. There are moots (meetings), workshops, discussion groups, and yearly events such as Éigse Spioraid Cheilteach - a gathering and celebration for all those with an interest in or currently practicing Celtic Spirituality and 'Nature-based' religions. (Details of current Irish contacts can be found in the Resources.)

So folks, there you have it. This, I hope, is the book I never had but always looked for, the book a lost and lonely 16-year-old searched the shelves of bookshops for, all those years ago; alas, in vain. I was looking for truth and integrity, I was looking for reality and practicality, I was looking for humor and honesty. I wanted Ireland in a mix of academia and accessibility, lore and laughter, earnestness and ease. I didn't find it at the time, but I truly hope you have.

This book is meant to be accessible enough for the lay or curious person, while still satisfying the driving need for historical accuracy among some of you more intensive scholars. The connection with the past is just as important as what we are experiencing today, and equally relevant is where we can possibly take things in the future. So many things have changed since I first wrote this book, but so much has remained the same. Honesty and respect are paramount. Personal experience has been shared; my soul lies bare in many places through these pages.

My original title for this book was True to the Heart, with the subtitle of 'Irish Witchcraft from an Irish Witch'. It was originally suggested to me by a friend at the time, and it rang so clearly and deeply with me that it was my first choice for this book. Its ambiguity got it vetoed by the original publisher, which is fair enough from a practical point of view. But I did want to include it here. Everything I have written in these pages is so close to my heart, I am filled with it every day. It's as true as I can make it, down to sacrificing the privacy of my own experiences to show you, Dear Reader, how the older traditions and beliefs can come about and follow through in a real-life setting. Truth has been vital in the writing of it. I offer you simply what I have seen and felt, and what those before have written and we can access. I have made it as clear as possible which is which, and what is what, and done my utmost to write that which I hold true to my heart.

In short, I have done my best with this book - then and now - though I myself am still seeking and learning, and will continue doing so for a very long time to come. I wanted to give you here what I felt and knew it means to be an Irish Witch. I hope you have enjoyed it.

Beannachtaí,
   Lora O'Brien

FIRST EDITION
   Bealtaine 2004
   Ros Comáin, Ireland

SECOND EDITION
   Lúnasa, 2020
   Port Láirge, Ireland

8

Resources

Bibliography

Following are books or papers that I have used as source material for this work, or have found to be useful and interesting in my continuing studies of Irish myths and legends, magic, Irish history, Witchcraft history, and Irish culture. It is a bit of a mixed list, apologies, I was not very thorough in citing sources when I first started out writing, and it has proven exceptionally difficulty to do it retrospectively!

As with all recommendations, take these not as gospel but as potentially useful aides. As an Amazon Associate I earn from qualifying purchases (I know, I know, but as an independent author and small press publisher it's a necessary evil). That means the following links are affiliate, so if you buy a book by copying or following a link, I may get a few cents per copy (at no cost to you). I have provided the most recent publisher info I could find, in case the links go out of date, or you want to search for the materials elsewhere.

Aleister Crowley
    Magick in Theory and Practice
    Albatross Publishers (February 9, 2018)

https://amzn.to/2XUxyl2

Aleister Crowley
  The Book of the Law
  Weiser Books; Reissue edition (May 1, 1987)
  https://amzn.to/2JLxCyF

Alexei Kondratiev
  Celtic Rituals
  New Celtic Pub.; This Edition (1999)
  https://amzn.to/2SjhBng

Barry Rafferty
  Pagan Celtic Ireland: The Enigma of the Irish Iron Age
  Thames and Hudson; 1st Edition edition (December 31, 1994)
  https://amzn.to/37Hwsjl

Brian P. Levack
  The Witch-Hunt in Early Modern Europe 4th Edition
  Routledge; 4 edition (October 6, 2015)
  https://amzn.to/2NKcvzU

Collins Press
  Collins Pocket Irish Dictionary
  HarperCollins UK; Fourth Edition (June 1, 2015)
  https://amzn.to/2JRWdBI

Dáithí Ó hÓgáin
  Myth, Legend, and Romance: An Encyclopaedia of Irish Folk Tradition
  Prentice Hall General; 1 edition (April 1, 1991)
  https://amzn.to/2JSowjM

Dáithí Ó hÓgáin

The Sacred Isle - Belief and Religion in Pre-christian Ireland
Boydell Press (October 4, 2001)
https://amzn.to/3fCMqOq

Eddie Lenihan
    In Search of Biddy Early
    From the Author: https://eddielenihan.weebly.com/store.html
    https://amzn.to/2UWzZoN

Joe McGowan
    Echoes of a Savage Land
    Mercier Press; 1St Edition edition (2001)
    https://amzn.to/3hMS82b

John-Paul Patton
    The Poet's Ogam: A Living Magical Tradition
    lulu.com (February 25, 2011)
    https://amzn.to/2LwUOmr

Jon O'Sullivan
    Tales of a Dagda Bard (Volumes One, Two and Three)
    Eel & Otter Press (2018, 2019, 2022)
    https://amzn.to/39hD3Se

Kuno Meyer
    The Voyage of Bran, Son of Febal, to the Land of the Living: An Old Irish
Saga (Classic Reprint)
    Forgotten Books (June 22, 2012)
    https://amzn.to/2xPqk7d

Máire MacNeill
    The Festival of Lughnasa: A Study of the Survival of the Celtic Festival of
the Beginning of Harvest

Folklore of Ireland Council (January 31, 2008)
https://amzn.to/31lRShX

Marian Green
The Gentle Arts Of Natural Magic
Thoth Publications; 2 edition (October 1, 1998)
https://amzn.to/2Ybgfja

Marian Green
The Complete Book of Aquarian Magic: A Practical Guide to the Magical
Arts
Weiser Books; Reprint edition (July 1, 2015)
https://amzn.to/3hu7dVf

Michael Scott
Irish Folk and Fairy Tales Omnibus Edition
Sphere; New Ed edition (August 24, 1989)
https://amzn.to/2qcwbn2

Morgan Daimler
Gods and Goddesses of Ireland: A Guide to Irish Deities
Moon Books (December 9, 2016)
https://amzn.to/30Wrm1k

Morgan Daimler
A New Dictionary of Fairies: A 21st Century Exploration of Celtic and
Related Western European Fairies
Moon Books; Reprint edition (March 1, 2020)
https://amzn.to/2ANJS11

Morgan Daimler
Irish Paganism: Reconstructing Irish Polytheism
Moon Books (October 30, 2015)

https://amzn.to/2YbN6nS

Nerys T. Patterson
Cattle Lords and Clansmen: The Social Structure of Early Ireland
University of Notre Dame Press (April 30, 1994)
https://amzn.to/2LRn6HU

Patrick F. Byrne
Witchcraft in Ireland (historical information)
(Paperback – January 1, 1969)
https://amzn.to/3edU7dF

Philip Heselton
Gerald Gardner And the Cauldron of Inspiration: An Investigation into
the Sources of Gardnerian Witchcraft
Holmes Pub Group Llc (November 30, 2003)
https://amzn.to/2LpURkT

Professor Ronald Hutton
The Triumph of the Moon: A History of Modern Pagan Witchcraft
Oxford University Press; 2 edition (December 1, 2019)
https://amzn.to/3edTq3L

Proinsias MacCana
Celtic Mythology
Hamlyn (1970)
https://amzn.to/2JNtGNI

Robert Magill Young, William Pinkerton, William O'Mellan
Historical Notices of Old Belfast and Its Vicinity
Franklin Classics (October 10, 2018)
https://amzn.to/2CKQN8I

Roseanne Schot (Editor), Conor Newman (Editor), Edel Bhreathnach (Editor)
Landscapes of cult and kingship
Four Courts Press (July 15, 2011)
https://amzn.to/302AfDU

St. John D. Seymour
Irish Witchcraft and Demonology
CreateSpace Independent Publishing Platform (November 24, 2013)
https://amzn.to/2CJiH4N

Thomas Cahill
How the Irish Saved Civilization: The Untold Story of Ireland's Heroic Role From the Fall of Rome to the Rise of Medieval Europe
Anchor; 1st edition (February 1, 1996)
https://amzn.to/30fEEBO

Thomas Kinsella
The Tain: Translated from the Irish Epic Tain Bo Cuailnge
Oxford University Press, U.S.A.; 1 edition (November 21, 2002)
https://amzn.to/30WymuW

W.Y. Evans-Wentz
The Fairy-Faith in Celtic Countries
CreateSpace Independent Publishing Platform (May 9, 2017)
https://amzn.to/2YbeZMY

PAPERS

- Alexei Kondratiev, 'An Tríbhís Mhór: The IMBAS Journal of Celtic Reconstructionism', Volume 2, issue 1/2, Samhain 1997/Iombolg 1998
- Françoise Le Roux, 'Le Dieu celtique aux liens de l'Ogmios de Lucien à l'Ogmios de Dürer', Ogam, 12 (1960), 209–34.

Online Sources

The Author's Blog and Website - Primarily focused on Irish Heritage, Culture and Paganism, the website provides a base for extensive resources and community networking. https://LoraOBrien.ie, and the FB Author page is at https://www.facebook.com/LoraOBrienInk

The Author's YouTube Channel - So. Many. Videos. *Please* check the playlists for themed resources on topics such as our Irish Language, the Mórrígan, Fairy and Folklore, Pagan Basics, the Ogham Language, Your Irish Connection Interviews, Readings of the Original Irish Source Lore, and so much more! https://www.youtube.com/user/loraobr

The Irish Pagan School (Pagan Education) – Online School providing authentic education from native Irish teachers, co-founded by the Author. There are *many* classes and programmes available, from free to fee paying. https://IrishPaganSchool.com

Eel & Otter Press - Irish Mythology Blog and Publisher (T-shirts, Mugs, Stickers) providing original designs based on our own symbols, quotes and phrases from Irish mythology, books and items, that we feel would be pleasing to our Irish Gods and Goddesses, co-founded by the Author. https://EelAndOtter.net

Pagan Life Rites (Irish Priesthood Organisation) – This is a non-profit organisation, operated cooperatively by a nationwide network of Priests and Priestesses, offering a range of services to the greater Pagan community of Ireland, co-founded by the Author. http://paganliferites.org

The Dagda Bard - Modern Irish storytelling blog from *An Scealaí Beag*, primarily focused on his Priesthood and relationship with the Chief God of the Tuatha Dé Danann, An Dagda. https://www.dagdabard.com

Brigid's Forge - A blog about Brigid, Irish deity, saint, nun, ollamh, and more, run by Irish Pagan Catholic writer and educator Orlagh Costello. https://mybrigidsforge.wordpress.com

Irish 101 - An Introduction to Irish Language and Culture, by Future learn at Dublin City University. Get an introduction to Ireland's culture by learning the basics of the Irish language. (This one is free, progressive courses are paid, but worth it!) https://www.futurelearn.com/courses/irish-language

Teanglann - Irish online dictionaries and language library, including grammar and pronunciation database guides. https://www.teanglann.ie/en/

(Please also check the Irish Pagan School for more Pagan specific Irish language learning)

JSTOR – This site provides access to more than 12 million academic journal articles, books, and primary sources in 75 disciplines. There's a free registration process now which gives you access to read up to six free articles a month, and organize sources and notes in your online workspace. https://www.jstor.org

CELT - University College Cork's Corpus of Electronic Texts online digitalisation project. List of Published Texts at https://celt.ucc.ie/publishd.html

Academia.edu – A platform for academics to share research papers, whose mission is "to accelerate the world's research". Over 65 million academics are on there, and around 21 million papers. There's paid options, but most of it is free. Check it. https://www.academia.edu

Pagan Federation (Networking and Activism) – They don't promote a single aspect or path within Paganism, nor do they presume to represent all

Pagans, but are an umbrella organisation with a membership drawn from all strands. http://www.paganfederation.org

Well of Wisdom – An Irish Pagan Temple based in Co. Cork. http://wellof wisdom.org

Witch (Minoan Brotherhood, and Traditional Wicca) – Irish, based in Asia. Run by a 3º High Priest of the Alexandrian Tradition of Wicca, with experience in the Minoan Brotherhood, the New York WICA Tradition and the Isian Tradition of Witchcraft. https://witch.ie

O.T.O. (Initiatory Fraternal Organisation) – Ordo Templi Orientis (O.T.O.) ('Order of the Temple of the East' or 'Order of Oriental Templars') is an international fraternal and religious organization, with it's roots in European Freemasonry. Historically, the leadership of this group have not been community service focused. https://www.oto.org

Janet Farrar and Gavin Bone – Wiccan authors and educators who live in County Meath, Ireland. Find them at Teampall na Callaighe. http://www.c allaighe.com

Kilkenny Druidry (Druid Priesthood) – Druid Grove run by Eimear Burke, the Chosen Chief of the Order of Bards, Ovates and Druids (OBOD); this is a resource for those wishing to connect to 'Celtic' source traditions. https://www.kilkennydruidry.com

Irish Shamanism – An Irish 'Shamanic' Community page for Native (Irish Celtic) Earth-based healing methods and spirituality. This Facebook Community is run by an Irish Priestess and Healer on https://www.facebo ok.com/groups/MidlandsCelticShamanism/

Barbara Lee Witch – Irish Facebook Page run by a Dublin based Alexandrian Wiccan High Priestess on https://www.facebook.com/BarbaraLeeW

itch/

Story Archaeology Podcast – Uncovering the layers of Irish Mythology. On this site, you will find a regular podcast and articles about Irish Pagan Mythology by the Story Archaeologists, Chris Thompson and Isolde Carmody. https://storyarchaeology.com/

Morgan Daimler - US based author and educator who provides exceptional Irish translation work, and a fantastic modern insight into relationship with the Irish Sidhe (the Fairies). Blog is at https://lairbhan.blogspot.com, Patreon is at https://www.patreon.com/morgandaimler.

Brigid's Forge – Irish Facebook Community dedicated to Brigid on https://www.facebook.com/groups/318562765289760/

The Dagda's Hearth – Irish Facebook Community dedicated to the Dagda on https://www.facebook.com/groups/Dagdashearth/

The Mórrígan's Cave – Irish Facebook Community dedicated to the Mórrígan on https://www.facebook.com/groups/MorrigansCave/

Learn Ogham - Irish Facebook Community dedicated to the study of Ogham on https://www.facebook.com/groups/LearnOgham

About the Author

Lora O'Brien is an Author, Teacher, and Guide: native born Irish, with 20+ years personal and professional experience in our history, heritage, archaeology, mythology, and pre-christian Irish Spirituality. Publications include - Irish Witchcraft from an Irish Witch, 2004; A Practical Guide to Irish Spirituality, 2013; Rathcroghan, A Journey, 2013; Tales of Old Ireland - Retold, 2018; Harp, Club and Cauldron, 2019; A Practical Guide to Pagan Priesthood, Llewellyn 2019; Irish Witchcraft - 2nd Edition, 2020; the Irish Queen Medb, 2020; and the Fairy Faith in Ireland, 2021.

She is a modern Draoí – a practitioner and priest of indigenous Irish magic and spirituality, in the simplest terms. Lora has been consciously following a pagan path for over 25 years, and dedicated specifically to the Irish Goddess Mórrígan in 2004. She managed one of Ireland's most important sacred sites - Cruachán/Rathcroghan - for a decade, and is a co-founder and legal celebrant with Pagan Life Rites Ireland.

With her partner, Jon O'Sullivan, she is the co-founder of the Irish Pagan School. Lora is currently a candidate for a Masters Degree in Irish Regional History (2023).

You can connect with me on:

- https://irishpaganschool.com
- https://twitter.com/LoraOB
- https://www.facebook.com/TheIrishPaganSchool
- https://loraobrien.ie
- https://www.youtube.com/c/TheIrishPaganSchool

Subscribe to my newsletter:

- https://forms.aweber.com/form/06/2015701906.htm

Also by Lora O'Brien

A Practical Guide to Pagan Priesthood

There's a pressing need in the Pagan community for strong, aware, responsible, and accountable leaders. This book provides a down-to-earth perspective on what it means to be a priestess or priest and explores the duties, responsibilities, challenges, and benefits of stepping into a leadership role.

Whether you are currently a priest or priestess, are considering taking on such a role, or would like to be more informed about Pagan leadership so you can better support your community, this book helps you learn about the practical skills required and provides ideas on how you can acquire or improve them.

Explore the two primary categories of priestly duties - pastoral and sacerdotal - and find a plethora of insight into specific topics, including group leadership, teaching, crisis counseling, communicating with deity, devotion to deity, intervention and healing, life rites, and community celebration. As Paganism continues to grow and new generations become leaders, this guide shares a practical picture of what the Pagan priesthood can be.

Tales of Old Ireland: Retold

In Ireland, we have a wealth of old myths, legends, fairy tales and folk stories, which are presented here in an easy to read, authentic Irish storyteller's voice - retold for modern times. Our Tales of Old Ireland reach from the heroic warriors Fionn and the Fianna, to the curse of a Goddess, to an on-going battle of wits between the Connacht Queen Medb (Maeve) and her rival the King of Ulster. You'll see shape shifting sisters, fairy folk you'll want to watch out for, fights with monsters, and wise old women helping young maids.

Rathcroghan, a Journey

The author's work as an Irish Heritage Professional is about connection; to Ireland's history, mythology, ancestry, sacred and everyday sites - all of this is communicated and passed on through Ireland's stories. This book is an expression of O'Brien's connection to 13 sites of the Rathcroghan Royal Complex, in County Roscommon - home of Queen Medb and the ancient Goddess Mórrígan - and the creative and intuitional inspiration that tells a story from each of those sites. Over 20 years of exploring Irish Spirituality, Lora O'Brien has learned to connect, and to find the story. Here she shares those stories with you - so join her, on a Rathcroghan Journey.

Harp, Club & Cauldron

He is a king, a druid, a war chieftain, a lover, and a worker of the land. He nourishes and he kills, he loves and he fights, in equal measure. He knows the sorcerous arts of druidry and the secrets of time. He is the Dagda - the mightiest of all the Irish Gods, and yet he is often overlooked in popular approaches to the Irish Gods. This book distills the scholarship, experience, and creative vision of the Irish and Celtic spirituality communities to bring you a harvest of knowledge featuring: — Works of original scholarship on the Dagda, his role in literature culture, and myth, and related divinities. — Translated early Irish textual material with commentary. — Tools for the practitioner including prayers, rituals, recipes. — Insightful experiential writings from priests and practitioners. — Curated original creative writings. — Original artwork and illustrations.No one reading this book will come away unsatisfied

A Practical Guide to Irish Pagan Spirituality

This book is about change, growth, learning, and connection. It is conversational, and informal, and a little bit fun to read. It is about looking at things around you – past, present, and future – and asking the important questions. Perhaps the only really important question: Why? This is a book for all of us who are looking, searching for a way to plant our feet firmly on Irish ground, and take responsibility for what we are doing here, for our place in the big picture that is Ireland today. You don't have to be Pagan, or New Age, or Magical, or Spiritual, to read this book. You don't even have to be Irish. To get the full benefit, you do have to be open minded, willing to learn something about yourself, about Ireland, and maybe even about your place in this land. This is also a practical guide and a work book, and that is important to understand before you buy. There are more questions within these pages than there are definitive answers. Understand that this work is up to you, and nobody else will take responsibility for the work you need to be doing. There is genuine guidance though, some funny bits, and more than a couple of pokes and prods to help you on your way. Written by a woman of this land, called Witch by some, Druid by others, and Bean Draoí by herself, when she has to go by something other than 'that O'Brien one'. Sharing experience and knowledge, and suggestions for how you might get to where you need to be – examining how things used to be done here, and what can be useful and relevant to us as we bring ourselves forward through our Irish Spirituality.

(New Edition Due 2022)

The Irish Queen Medb: History, Tradition, and Modern Pagan Practice
It is told throughout the lands that the jealousy, spite, and arrogance, of Ireland's Queen Medb started the great battle of the Táin Bó Cuailgne (Cattle Raid of Cooley). But is this accurate? Is this the true story of Medb?

Examining this historical and mythological figure - with the guidance of a native expert in Irish heritage and spirituality - exposes a tangled web of cultural context which is missing from most of her tales. While the commonly available stories seem to focus only on the faults and foibles of the ruler of the western province, Connacht, from her seat at Cruachan (Rathcroghan), this work takes us on a deep dive through the core aspects of the information that is available about the Irish Queen - or Goddess - Medb (Maeve), so we can see what was really going on.

Peppering the book with direct quotes and authentic snippets from the original manuscript source lore, the author also explains and expands upon these often dense and occasionally confusing texts, in ways which make the material approachable and understandable. Given this firm foundation, along with the sharing of unique and personal experiences throughout Ireland at the sites most sacred to Medb, the reader can easily follow where the author has walked. This is a path that leads to solid spiritual connection within a modern Pagan practice, guided by a native Irish Draoí.

The Fairy Faith in Ireland: History, Tradition, and Modern Pagan Practice

Do we believe in Fairies? Really?

The Fairy Faith in Ireland has a long history, from the time of the Tuatha Dé Danann through the coming of Christianity, with many traditions continuing still to this day. These beliefs and practices have been studied by many scholars, antiquarians, and folklorists, and subsequently been picked up and popularised by Neo Pagan authors. We hear often now of Irish Fairies or the Sidhe being used in New Age 'Celtic Fairy Witchcraft' systems or beliefs.

Unfortunately, the majority of those who have been researching and writing about the Fairy Faith in Ireland for centuries, and those who have been attempting to practice the faith in a modern context, have been outside the culture. This has led to much misunderstanding and misappopriation of the ways we have always dealt with the Fairies in Ireland.

In this book you will learn the truth about Fairies, as we believe it in Ireland. Through these pages you will discover...
  - What is a Fairy?
  - Who are the Different Types of Fairies?
  - Where do we Find Fairies?
  - How to Spot Fairy Behaviour and Misbehaviour?
  - How to Stay Safe from the Fairies?

'The Fairy Faith in Ireland: History, Tradition, and Modern Pagan Practice' is written from the perspective of a native Irish Draoí (Druid and Priestess of the Old Gods), who has been raised in Ireland immersed in the mythology, folklore, and practical experiences in which our culture is so rich. The author went on to study, teach and write on these topics from 1994 to present day, having her first book published in 2004. She developed a professional career in Irish Heritage tourism and management, having the

196

honour of guiding people through an authentic connection experience for many decades. She co-founded Pagan Life Rites Ireland to support legitimate and legal practice of our native spiritual beliefs, and the Irish Pagan School to provide a platform for a community of Irish voices to teach and share the collective wisdom of our people. This is the 8th book Lora O'Brien has written/edited, and she is currently a candidate for a Masters Degree in Irish Regional History (2023).

Do we believe in Fairies? Yes we really do.
   Do you?!

Buy The Fairy Faith in Ireland today to find your own answers, based on genuine information and experience.

Made in the USA
Middletown, DE
12 August 2023

36624187R00142